TRAIN YOUR MIND

Tibetan Exercises in
Wisdom and Compassion

DHIRANANDA & VIRYABODHI

Windhorse Publications
38 Newmarket Road
Cambridge CB5 8DT
info@windhorsepublications.com
windhorsepublications.com

© Dhirananda and Viryabodhi 2023

© Windhorse Publications 2025

The right of Dhirananda and Viryabodhi to be identified as the authors of this work has been asserted by them in accordance with the Copyright, Designs and Patents Act 1988.

No portion of this book may be utilised in any form for the training, development, enhancement, or operation of any artificial intelligence technologies. This prohibition includes all forms of AI, including generative models, neural networks, and any other types of computational intelligence. This restriction extends to all methods of obtaining or utilising data, including but not limited to data scraping, data mining, direct or indirect observation, manual entry, or any innovative data sourcing techniques that might be developed in the future.

For General Product Safety Regulation (EU) queries, the authorized representative for Windhorse Publications Ltd is:
Buddhistisches Tor Berlin
Buddhistische Gemeinschaft Triratna (Berlin) E.V.
Grimmstrasse 11B-C
10967 Berlin-Kreuzberg
info@buddhistisches-tor-berlin.de

Cover design by Katarzyna Manecka
Typesetting by Tarajyoti

British Library Cataloguing in Publication Data:
A catalogue record for this book is available from the British Library.

ISBN 978-1-915342-51-5

Cover image: Created by Alexandre Westerlund, with the help of Leonardo.ai

Praise for *Train Your Mind: Tibetan Exercises in Wisdom and Compassion*

This book is precious. Read it carefully to discover a brilliant map for training your mind and heart that is immediately applicable to all of life's circumstances. If things are going well, be generous and share your good fortune. If things are difficult, use this as an opportunity for empathy for others suffering in similar ways. Treat challenges and difficulties as opportunities. Hold all of your life lightly. Be brave. Be kind.

This is the approach of the wonderful lojong tradition from Mahayana and Tibetan Buddhism. Dhirananda and Viryabodhi have done a brilliant job of translating the profound and compassionate slogans from the seven-point mind training into immediately accessible and practical teachings for the modern world. This book is a wonderful offering that shows the depth of their practice, as well as their ability to communicate wise and subtle teachings in a clear and straightforward way.

In many ways this book contains the quintessential teachings for our troubled times, and I heartily encourage you to read it and put the teachings into practice in your life. – **Vidyamala Burch OBE**, founder of the Breathworks Foundation and author of *Living Well with Pain and Illness*, *Mindfulness for Health*, and *Mindfulness for Women*

Based on teachings that originated in eleventh-century Tibet, Dhirananda and Viryabodhi have produced a contemporary treasure house of advice for cultivating a heart and mind of compassion and wisdom. This is a book of clarity and depth for transforming adversities into occasions for insight, packed with suggestions for daily practice and reflection. – **Vaddhaka Linn**, author of *The Buddha on Wall Street: What's Wrong with Capitalism and What We Can Do about It*

The pithy slogans of the Tibetan mind-training tradition challenge us to face up to our self-centredness and to recognize how it perpetuates our suffering. Here is a practically grounded addition to the growing body of literature on this profound set of teachings. While drawing on several traditional commentaries, the authors show how this ancient wisdom remains pertinent to today's existential challenges. – **Nagapriya**, author of *The Promise of a Sacred World: Shinran's Teaching of Other Power*

This is a great book for anyone who wants to know how to practise the Dharma in every moment of their life. The authors are excellent guides, who write in a clear but friendly way. They invite us to change our habitual attitudes to ones in which we treat whatever happens to us as gifts – opportunities to grow spiritually. – **Ratnaguna**, author of *The Art of Reflection* and *Great Faith, Great Wisdom*

Buddhism is about training the mind. Lojong, which literally means 'mind training' in Tibetan, includes pointers on how we can use life's inevitable setbacks and see them as opportunities for change. It's a wonderful idea: that we can turn difficulties and problems into tools to help us develop and become increasingly free. Lojong emphasizes that we must transform our relationships with others and cultivate deep compassion. My two friends have exemplified this compassion by producing this skilfully crafted book. – **Dharmachari Sona**, senior member of the Triratna Buddhist Order

Contents

	Authors' Acknowledgements	vii
	Publisher's Acknowledgements	viii
	Audio Recordings	ix
	Foreword	xi
	Introduction	1
	The Seven Points and the Fifty-Nine Slogans	11
Point One:	Preparations	15
Point Two:	Absolute and Relative Bodhicitta	23
Point Three:	Turning Difficulties into Means of Awakening	47
Point Four:	Synthesis: Practice for a Whole Life	63
Point Five:	Measuring the Effects of Our Practice	71
Point Six:	Specific Commitments in Relation to Others	79
Point Seven:	Guidelines for Lojong	99
	Conclusion	127
	Links to Other Mind-Training Resources	129
	Notes and References	131

Authors' Acknowledgements

We would like to express our deepest gratitude to our teachers: Sangharakshita, Vessantara, Sona, Subhuti, and many others. We would also like to thank everyone who participated in the retreats we led on the lojong theme, as well as all those who so generously contributed to the production of the Swedish edition, including Alexandre Westerlund (cover and layout) and Jenny Norman (copy-editing). We would also like to express our gratitude to Windhorse Publications for the courage to publish an English edition of the book, and in particular Dhammamegha as the director for your warm enthusiasm and encouragement.

The annotated text of the lojong slogans is written by Dhirananda; reflections, exercises, and meditations are written by Viryabodhi.

Publisher's Acknowledgements

We would like to thank the individuals who donated through our 'Sponsor-a-book' campaign. You can find out more about it at https://www.windhorsepublications.com/sponsor-a-book/.

Windhorse Publications wish to gratefully acknowledge a grant from the Future Dharma Fund and the Triratna European Chairs' Assembly Fund towards the production of this book.

Audio Recordings

Train Your Mind has been produced with accompanying guided meditations by the authors.

They are indicated by this image:

These can be streamed directly from the web.

Please go to: https://www.windhorsepublications.com/free-resources/tym-audio/

Foreword

I discovered Buddhism and meditation as a young medical student in the early 1980s. I went mountain climbing and, during a dramatic multi-day climb in the USA, I had my first real close encounter with my own mortality. After that, I found it difficult to expose myself to the same kind of dangers and challenges. At the same time, I was not really in touch with the feeling of how valuable this life is. Without these adventures, life felt empty somehow.

Buddhism replaced physical challenge with deeper interest, excitement, and meaning. I met Sona, an English Buddhist who had moved to Sweden, and through him I became involved in what was then known as the Friends of the Western Buddhist Order, or FWBO (VBV in Swedish). It was a movement started by an Englishman who had spent twenty years in India as a monk. Sangharakshita was ordained as a *bhikkhu* in the Theravada tradition, but most of his teachers were Tibetan lamas who had fled Tibet after the Chinese occupation, and whom he met in Kalimpong. One of his main teachers was also a Zen Buddhist.

I was attracted by the way Sangharakshita drew inspiration from all Buddhist schools and showed how they were all expressions of the Buddhist ideal of enlightenment. His encyclopedic knowledge included not only the entire Buddhist tradition but also Western philosophy, art, and literature. The FWBO later changed its name to Triratna, which in a way was a pity, as the link to Western cultural heritage became less explicit.

Sangharakshita's presentation of the Dharma, the Buddha's teachings, has been fundamental to my own understanding of Buddhism. But my interest in lojong was only sparked much later, in the summer of 2018. I was on a retreat with Vessantara, a member of the Order I got to know in 1982 during my own ordination retreat. Vessantara, together with his partner Vijayamala, had completed a three-year retreat in France, guided by Lama Tilmann Lhundrup. Much of the initial phases of their retreat had focused on lojong.

An important reason why I took up the lojong teachings at this time was that I was going through a difficult period where several of my loved ones were seriously ill. Both my parents developed Alzheimer's disease a few years apart and eventually passed away. As a practising GP, I was of course used to dealing with illness and death. But, during these years, I encountered personal suffering in a way I hadn't before.

What appeals to me most about lojong is the emphasis on how to face difficulties in life as a means of awakening. And lojong can be practised in *all* circumstances. No matter what the demands of life and how busy you are, you can reflect on any of the slogans in lojong and draw strength and inspiration from them.

It has been a bonus to work on this project with Viryabodhi, my friend and brother in the Order for many years. Viryabodhi has helped me to edit and improve what I have written, while the sections he has written have helped to create a more readable and useful book.

Foreword

I am now retired from medical work, and spend my time reading and writing and enjoying nature and the outdoors. During the summer I spend as much time as I can at our country house in Roslagen with my dear Lena and our children when they want to come here. This book would not be what it is without my family. They have often been in my thoughts when I have written and, together with Lena, I have often meditated and reflected on the slogans in lojong.

Dhirananda
Vaxholm, Sweden
August 2024

* * *

I first came into contact with the lojong teachings in 2004, on a retreat led by Sona for Nordic Order members of Triratna in Finland. The theme was the 'eight verses of mind training' by the Tibetan teacher Geshe Langri Tangpa. These verses belong to the same tradition as the slogans in this book. Sona had studied these verses with Subhuti, another senior member of the Order, on a retreat earlier that year.

The retreat in Finland lived on in our practice in various ways, but above all in a slogan that read: 'All beings are extremely kind' – not just kind but *extremely* kind, even the difficult ones. The phrase became part of our sangha culture, popped up in the teaching at the Stockholm Buddhist Centre, and was eventually printed on T-shirts: *All beings are extremely kind*, together with a lotus flower and underneath it, in small script, *Stockholms Buddhistcenter*. This slogan gives a flavour of the challenging teachings found in lojong.

Foreword

Sona was the first member of the Order I met when I attended a meditation and puja in autumn of 1982, and he eventually became an important role model and spiritual friend. Subhuti was a close friend of Sona's, and also became an important teacher and role model to me, as well as the one who in 1989 ordained me and gave me my Buddhist name, Viryabodhi (which means 'energy in pursuit of enlightenment').

The first time I came into contact with Dhirananda was actually in his absence during that autumn of 1982, when he was on his ordination retreat in Tuscany. I remember being thrilled when I heard about it. That you could do something like that made an impression on me. The second time I met Dhirananda was during a summer retreat that he led in 1985, supported by Sona. The retreat took place at Stenfors, in the south of Sweden. The theme of this retreat was the Bodhisattva Ideal. Among other things, I remember that we sat in a large circle and read from a text about this ideal and about the bodhisattva, who can be said to be an ideal Buddhist who strives for enlightenment not only for themselves but for the sake of all beings. One evening, Dhirananda asked me to read a whole chapter from the book *A Guide to the Bodhisattva's Way of Life* (*The Bodhicaryavatara*) – in English. Strangely, the chapter was about virya ('energy in the pursuit of good'). It was as if he had a premonition of what was in store for me in a few years. At that time, I did yoga for two or three hours every day and certainly had a lot of energy. As a matter of fact, I had been invited to teach yoga on the retreat.

One can often discern threads of teaching that run through the Buddhist tradition over time and manifest in slightly different ways. Most of them were already present in the teachings of Gautama Buddha. One such thread is the teaching of loving-kindness, metta, both in the main text of this teaching, the *Karaniyametta-sutta*, and in the meditation known as *metta-bhavana* ('the development of loving-kindness').[1] In that meditation, one cultivates loving-kindness and care for oneself, and then for a friend, a neutral person, a difficult person, and finally all living beings.

The teachings on metta later blossomed into bodhicitta, the wish for enlightenment for the sake of all beings, and into the ideal of the bodhisattva in Mahayana Buddhism. An important text, which is also one of the Dalai Lama's favourite texts, is precisely the *Guide to the Bodhisattva's Way of Life* that I mentioned earlier. In my view, the teachings we find in lojong are part of this thread, and also intertwined with a lot of other teachings that can be traced back, if you like.

Within the Triratna tradition that Dhirananda and I belong to, the lojong teachings have also been present through Sangharakshita's contact with his Tibetan teachers, and in a more direct way since the early 2000s. At that time, many Order members began exploring lojong in earnest, both the seven-point mind training and fifty-nine slogans that you find in this book and the eight verses of mind training. At the end of the book you will find tips on some of the teachings in Triratna that came out of this exploration. Someone who has explored lojong and practises it in her own life is Vidyamala, founder of Breathworks and recipient of the Order of the British Empire for her work with people living with chronic pain and other difficulties

Foreword

(through mindfulness and self-compassion). She combines the practice of awareness (*satipatthana*) with lojong, and has led several retreats on this theme.

Sangharakshita himself had plans to give teachings on lojong, but this never materialized. However, traces of it can be found in a study seminar he gave on a text, *Precepts of the Gurus*, which contains the teachings of Atisha and his followers in Tibet.

When Dhirananda approached me and other friends a few years ago and suggested that we organize a week-long retreat on lojong in the summer of 2021, we happily agreed. By then, he had already written most of the material you find in this book in Swedish. During the retreat we started talking about making a book out of the text, and immediately started working on it. In the spring of 2022, I took the material on a solitary retreat at Adelsö, and carefully went through the text. I took notes and wrote up suggestions for reflections and guided meditations that could be added. At the same time, Dhirananda produced a deck of Swedish lojong cards, with a card for each of the fifty-nine slogans and a short introduction, and had a first edition of 200 copies printed.

It has been a joy to work with Dhirananda on the book, with many Zoom meetings and real-life meetings as well. This is not the first time that Dhirananda has immersed himself in something in this way and written down his reflections and his own understanding, but it is the first time that these have been turned into a book. Now more people will have the opportunity to benefit from his subtle insights and creative ability to summarize and express sometimes very difficult thoughts and teachings.

Foreword

We hope that you will enjoy and benefit from this appealing and challenging teaching in your own practice and in your everyday life. It would be great to hear from you about your experience of the book and the training.

Viryabodhi
Maitrigiri community
Enskede, Sweden
August 2024

Introduction

Lojong, or 'training the mind in seven points', is a classic teaching of Tibetan Buddhism. It is a kind of manual on the art of developing and practising wisdom and compassion. The version of lojong presented here consists of fifty-nine slogans, each of which conveys an attitude towards life that aims to change our habitual way of thinking, communicating, and acting. Instead of being constantly motivated by self-interest, the slogans encourage us to think, communicate, and act primarily in the interests and for the well-being of others.

Lojong is a guide or manual on how to develop and broaden our compassion. But it is also a guide on how to develop the wisdom that is a prerequisite for all-encompassing universal compassion. As humans, we have an innate ability to be compassionate towards other humans, but also towards living beings that do not belong to our own species. Throughout evolution, our ability as humans to cooperate with and care for each other, even the weak and defenceless in the herd, has been important for our survival. We take care of our children who for many years lack the ability to survive on their own, but we also take care of members of the pack who are old and sick. The ability to appreciate altruistic acts can be observed already in infants.

The capacity for compassion has historically been limited to the family, clan, or pack. Presumably, even this limitation in our capacity for compassion has had a survival value. But it has also created much of the suffering that has characterized our history to date: conflicts, violence, war, mass extinction of animal and plant species, exploitation of nature, and ecological imbalance, which now even threatens all life on the planet.

Working to reduce limitations and instead increase our ability to be compassionate towards other living beings can therefore be seen as a crucial factor for our collective survival. Compassion for others means learning to recognize and experience the suffering of others. It also involves a strong desire to reduce suffering and a willingness to do what one can to alleviate it.

In the Buddhist tradition, compassion is the starting point. For the goal of Buddhist training is the cessation of suffering. The Buddha himself recognized that there are two kinds of suffering in life. One kind of suffering is inevitable. Being embodied, we will fall ill, get injured, grow old, and eventually die. Suffering associated with such natural life processes can therefore not be avoided.

But we *can* avoid a large part of our collective suffering. This is the suffering we unnecessarily inflict on others and thereby indirectly on ourselves. It is also suffering we create in addition to our already existing suffering through our attitude to what happens in our lives. When we recognize and understand how our attitude influences our level of suffering, we can learn to reduce suffering for ourselves and others by getting to the root of the causes of this 'subjective' suffering.

Lojong is a collection of teachings in Tibetan Buddhism. The word *lo* means 'mind', or 'attitude' in Tibetan, and *jong* means 'training'. So 'lojong' can be translated as 'training the

Introduction

mind', or 'training our attitude'. The most fundamental shift in attitude that the training seeks to achieve is to reduce our self-centredness and instead open us up to how others feel. This means moving from an 'I' to a 'we', and ultimately to a 'we' that knows no boundaries – a movement from an 'I and they', or a 'we and they', until finally there is only a 'we and we'.

Although lojong originated in Tibetan Buddhism, its message is universal and timeless. Throughout all times and all cultures, people seeking self-realization have discovered that the highest form of self-realization involves *transcending the self*. It is only by going beyond the narrow interests of the self that we find true happiness and fulfilment. As long as we are trapped within the limited horizon of self-identification, we create suffering for ourselves and for others.

Buddhism was introduced to Tibet in several phases. The first began around 650 CE when the first king of a unified Tibet, Songtsän Gampo, tried to introduce Buddhism. He established several monasteries, but found it difficult to gain popular support for the new teachings. Then, 140 years later, King Thrisong Detsen continued the efforts to consolidate Buddhist teachings among the Tibetans. He invited several renowned teachers from India. Chief among them was the tantric master and yogi Padmasambhava, later considered by many Tibetans to be a second buddha and revered as much as Gautama Buddha, the historical Buddha.

Padmasambhava is regarded as the founder of the Nyingma, the oldest school of Tibetan Buddhism, whose teachings are largely based on *termas*, texts that Padmasambhava is said to have hidden, and which have been 'found' at various times throughout history by special people called *tertöns*.

In the mid-eighth century, Buddhism suffered a setback when Tibet had a new king, Langdharma, who was openly hostile to the religion. Langdharma was assassinated, but in the aftermath Buddhist institutions were severely damaged and the Tibetan empire disintegrated due to infighting.

It was only towards the end of the tenth century that Buddhism in Tibet was revitalized. Indian teachers were again invited to teach and build up the monastic system.

The most famous of these teachers was Atisha, who was invited in 1042 by the Tibetan king Yeshe-Ö. Atisha was the son of a Bengali king, but, like Siddhartha Gautama, he abandoned the privileged life at court. He was ordained as a monk at the age of twenty-nine, and quickly became famous for his extensive learning and mastery of tantric teachings.

According to Tibetan sources, Atisha spent twelve years in Sumatra, where he studied under a master named Dharmakirti, or Serlingpa as he is also called by Tibetans. After returning to India, he was appointed abbot of the renowned monastic university of Vikramashila.

At the age of sixty, Atisha was invited to Tibet. Despite his age and the knowledge that the harsh climate and living conditions in Tibet would probably shorten his life, he decided to accept. It is said that, before leaving, he thought that the Tibetans would be an easy-going people and that he would not have enough challenges. He therefore chose to take a companion, a monk who was known for his awkward temper. Once in Tibet, however, he soon realized that the Tibetans were difficult enough to give him challenges.

Atisha's importance to Tibetan Buddhism can only be compared to that of Padmasambhava. While Padmasambhava,

Introduction

who worked in the seventh century, represents above all the tantric guru who magically converted the native gods and demons, Atisha represents a mature balance of learning, meditative insight, and yogic perfection.

Atisha mastered all aspects of medieval Indian Buddhism, which was characterized by Mahayana Buddhism and tantra. But he chose to reduce the tantric element in the teachings that he gave to the Tibetans at this time. Central to his teaching was bodhicitta, the will to awaken for all beings' sake, which is one of the cornerstones of Mahayana Buddhism.

Bodhicitta is grounded in compassion, but signifies compassion in a broader and deeper sense than what we usually associate with the term. It is an all-encompassing compassion that includes both wisdom and love. According to Buddhism, wisdom and love are not separate. When we see reality as it is, when we see that we do not exist as discrete, separate individuals, but are interdependent with all living beings, ultimately with all that exists, love is the natural and spontaneous response to that realization.

Compassion in this sense, known in Buddhism as bodhicitta, can be divided into two aspects: absolute and relative.

Absolute bodhicitta corresponds to wisdom and insight into shunyata, or emptiness. When Buddhists say that everything is emptiness, it does not mean that nothing exists. Rather, it means that everything is empty of something that we believe exists in everything we perceive, namely a fixed and independent nature, an essence. When we see a horse or a tree, we think that is exactly what we are seeing, a horse or a tree. But Buddhism asks us to look a little closer. What are we really seeing? We see light and patterns and movements that we interpret. We label what we see and then think we know what it is. Often our interpretations of what we see agree with the interpretations of others, and all is well from an everyday, practical point of view.

But other times we misinterpret or read too much into what we experience, creating problems for ourselves and others. We react emotionally to what we think are facts about the world, and come into conflict with other people and the world we live in. But things do not exist 'from their own side', as the Tibetans put it. Instead, different phenomena arise according to certain conditions, and cease as soon as those conditions cease. Everything exists in an interdependent relationship with other factors. It is only in our own consciousness that the phenomena become things that we clearly recognize.

Instead of talking about emptiness, we can talk about *openness*. To see the emptiness of existence is to see the total openness of everything that exists. Talking about the openness of existence really has the same meaning as when we talk about the emptiness of existence, but it gives us completely different emotional associations.

The second aspect of bodhicitta is relative bodhicitta, which corresponds to compassion as an active feeling and motivation to action. According to Mahayana Buddhism, wisdom and compassion are two sides of the same coin. To see the emptiness and interdependence of all that exists is to experience an all-encompassing compassion.

Lojong is a concise and pithy teaching on bodhicitta inspired by Atisha. It is usually formulated in fifty-nine short slogans, which are easy to remember and serve as pointers to important aspects of the practice.

Introduction

Atisha's foremost disciple, Dromtönpa, passed on the teachings and founded the influential Kadam school. Dromtönpa's disciple Chekawa then wrote down the lojong teachings, while dividing the fifty-nine slogans into seven points, or sections, for pedagogical reasons. Lojong is therefore often referred to as 'training the mind in seven points' or seven-point mind training.

It is said that one day in his monastery Geshe Chekawa saw a written sentence that made a great impression on him. The sentence read: 'Give all victory to others, take all loss onto yourself.'

The meaning was so overwhelming for him that he tried every way to find out the origin of the sentence and have it explained. Eventually he found out that it was his own teacher, Sharawa, who had written it. He learned that it was part of a secret transmission from teacher to student. Most monks were not particularly interested in this message, but, for those who truly aspired to insight and awakening, it was an indispensable teaching.

Over time, lojong has been adopted by all the Buddhist schools in Tibet and has gained enormous popularity. With the growing interest in Tibetan Buddhism and the increasing number of Westerners practising the Dharma, interest in lojong has also increased significantly in the West in recent times.

Central to the practice of lojong is the meditation known in Tibetan as tonglen, which means 'giving and receiving'. Tonglen involves meditating on compassion with a focus on the breath. Before one engages with the practice, one goes through a few preparatory stages, beginning with going for refuge to the Three Jewels (the Buddha, Dharma, and Sangha).

After this, one connects with the Buddha or a particular buddha or bodhisattva, imagining them above one or within one's heart. It is easy to become overwhelmed if you think you have to somehow transform all suffering by yourself. Having connected with something bigger than you, you can then imagine that you breathe in unhealthy influences such as greed, hatred, and ignorance, and breathe out healing and healthy influences such as generosity, love, and wisdom. (Under points seven and ten and in the following guided tonglen meditation, we go into tonglen in more detail.)

The combination of slogans that range from profound metaphysical teachings to practical advice for everyday life makes lojong an exceptionally rich and all-encompassing practice. Lojong is also particularly suitable for those who do not have the opportunity to live as a monk or nun, but have (worldly) responsibilities such as work and family and thus limited opportunities for serious and secluded meditation. A starting point for lojong is that all activities, no matter how mundane or 'worldly' they may seem, can be included in our practice and training in compassion. Setbacks and difficulties, which are inevitable, are no exception. On the contrary, they give us even better opportunities for training in compassion than when things are going well.

Sources

Several of the most prominent Buddhist teachers of our time have written translations and commentaries on lojong in English.

Introduction

The classic interpretation and commentary on lojong was written by Jamgön Kongtrül (1813–99), translated into English by Ken McLeod.[2]

Jamgön Kongtrül was one of the foremost teachers in Tibet in the nineteenth century and the founder of the Rimé movement, which endeavoured to unite the various Buddhist traditions in Tibet.

Another prominent Tibetan teacher who interpreted lojong is Dilgo Khyentse Rinpoche (1910–91).[3]

Dilgo Khyentse was one of the most prominent lamas who fled Tibet after the Chinese takeover in 1959. He belonged to the Nyingma tradition but, like Jamgön Kongtrül, was an advocate of the Rimé movement. He first settled in Bhutan, invited by the royal family to work and teach there. From 1980 he was based in Kathmandu, where he taught scores of lamas, disciples, and students from all over the world.

Perhaps one of the most important promoters of lojong in the West was Chögyam Trungpa (1939–87), connected to both the Kagyu and the Nyingma traditions and the founder of the Shambala tradition based in the United States. Following Chögyam Trungpa, several of his disciples, including Pema Chödrön and Judy Lief, have written commentaries on lojong.[4]

Alan Wallace, who has served for many years as an interpreter for many Tibetan teachers, including the Dalai Lama, has produced a translation of the lojong teachings with a commentary based on a number of authoritative sources, in the form of both oral teachings from Tibetan teachers and original texts not previously translated into English.[5]

Traleg Kyabgon (1955–2012), a prominent lama of the Kagyu tradition, has also written a translation of the lojong slogans with a commentary.[6] In addition to his deep familiarity with the wisdom tradition of Tibetan Buddhism, Traleg Kyabgon was also well versed in Western philosophy. His experience of teaching Westerners for more than twenty years enabled him to highlight those aspects of lojong that are particularly relevant to our times.

An interesting angle on lojong is given by Zoketsu Norman Fischer, a poet and Zen Buddhist who teaches at the San Francisco Zen Centre.[7] His often freer interpretations of the lojong slogans emphasize their universality and authenticity.

We have used all these sources and tried to find formulations that do justice to the slogans, first in Swedish and then in English. Many times we have had to choose between a formally more correct formulation that requires a lot of explanation and a simpler formulation that speaks for itself. Most often we have chosen the latter. Lojong is a kind of manual for daily practice. It is therefore more important that the slogans speak to you and serve as a source of inspiration than that they are 100 per cent faithful to the Tibetan original.

Anyone interested in learning more about lojong is strongly encouraged to read more of the extensive commentarial literature on the subject.

This book is an invitation to a journey that may well be long and rewarding. The most important thing is not the knowledge that can be conveyed in writing, but the experience that reflection and meditation on the slogans can provide. Once you understand the spirit of lojong, you will find your own formulations and perhaps create some of your own slogans based on your own life and experience.

The Seven Points and the Fifty-Nine Slogans

Point one: preparations

1. Start with the preparations.

Point two: absolute and relative bodhicitta

Absolute bodhicitta
2. Think of things as dreamlike.
3. Explore the nature of unborn awareness.
4. Let even the antidote free itself.
5. Rest in alaya, the fundamental nature of all experiences.
6. Between meditations, play with the illusions.

Relative bodhicitta
7. Practise giving and receiving alternately. Place them on the breath.
8. Three types of objects, three poisons, three seeds of goodness.
9. Practise using slogans in all activities.
10. Start giving and receiving with yourself.

Point three: turning difficulties into means of awakening

11. When the world is filled with evil, transform all unfavourable conditions into means of awakening.
12. Blame it all on the one culprit.
13. Be grateful to everyone.
14. Seeing both confusion and awakening as emptiness is the ultimate protection.
15. Do good, purify your mind, make peace with the demons, and ask for help.
16. Whenever you encounter something unexpected, combine it with meditation.

Point four: synthesis: practice for a whole life

17. Make the most of your life: practise the five strengths.
18. Also practise for the moment of death.

Point five: measuring the effects of our practice

19. All Dharma teaching is based on one thing.
20. Of the two witnesses, stick to the most important one.
21. Always keep a joyful mind.
22. You are well trained if you can practise even when distracted.

Introduction

Point six: specific commitments in relation to others

23. Stick to the three basic principles at all times.
24. Change your attitude but stay natural.
25. Don't talk about other people's defects.
26. Don't speculate on the intentions of others.
27. Work on the main poisons first.
28. Drop all expectations of results.
29. Avoid toxic foods.
30. Don't be so predictable.
31. Don't speak ill of others.
32. Don't ambush others.
33. Don't push things to the point of pain.
34. Don't put the burden of a dzo on an ox.
35. Don't strive to be first to the top.
36. Don't act with an ulterior motive.
37. Don't turn gods into demons.
38. Don't exploit the misfortune of others for your own benefit.

Point seven: guidelines for lojong

39. Do everything with the same purpose.
40. Meet all opposition with the same intention.
41. Two activities: one at the beginning and one at the end.
42. Whichever of the two occurs, remain patient.
43. Watch these two, even at the risk of your life.
44. Practise the three difficulties.
45. Create the three main conditions.

46. Make sure the three never subside.
47. Keep the three inseparable.
48. Train without one-sidedness in all respects. It is crucial to do it comprehensively and wholeheartedly.
49. Always meditate on what causes bitterness.
50. Don't be influenced by external circumstances.
51. At this crucial time, practise the essentials.
52. Beware of misplaced emotions.
53. Do not waver.
54. Train wholeheartedly.
55. Free yourself by examining and analyzing.
56. Don't feel sorry for yourself.
57. Don't be touchy.
58. Don't be frivolous.
59. Don't expect applause.

Point One

Preparations

Slogan One: Start with the Preparations

Training in wisdom and compassion in the systematic and comprehensive way of lojong is like being on a long and sometimes demanding journey. On it, we will face unforeseen difficulties and walk through unfamiliar territory.

As with any long journey, preparation is crucial. It helps to get a good idea of where we are going. For this we need maps and guidebooks. We need to pack all the equipment we might need. We also need to prepare ourselves mentally, and be motivated to deal with the inevitable problems and inconveniences we will face.

To begin, we need to recognize and understand the goal of the training, which is to develop an all-embracing compassion. The equipment includes qualities such as openness, curiosity, and a willingness to learn. It is crucial that we actually believe in the possibility of change, that it is possible to become more compassionate at all. If we believe that the capacity to be compassionate is something innate that we either have or don't have, we will find it difficult to motivate ourselves to practise.

We also need to gather all the courage, stamina, and willpower we can muster to embark on a journey into the unknown. Because, although training in compassion sounds safe and reliable, lojong involves such a radical change in our basic attitude to life and ourselves that we time and again will feel quite challenged and perhaps even vulnerable.

According to the tradition, there are four things to reflect on before starting – four basic and motivating facts about life that prepare you for lojong practice.

The unique opportunity that this life presents

What is the probability that a planet like Earth would come into being, with all the conditions necessary for life to emerge? What is the probability that organic life, once established on Earth, would evolve into beings as complex as you and me? And what is the likelihood that it is you and I who would be here now, having this conversation?

Life is such a unique gift that it is simply unimaginable. We all realize this in certain moments. But we forget it and become blasé and cynical about our lives. Or we get so caught up in our personal suffering that we fail to recognize the uniqueness and wonder of being alive right now.

We can remind ourselves of the unique opportunity that this life gives us, again and again. It is amazing just to be alive and aware. It is even more amazing that we have the opportunity to explore life and consciousness and try to understand what is really important in life.

The inevitability of death and decay

Something that further emphasizes the importance of seeing life as a unique gift is the knowledge that our time is limited. We know that we are living now, but not whether we will live tomorrow, or next week or next month. Therefore, there is no time to waste. What is most important in life we must do now. And, in order to have the time and opportunity to do what is most important, we must, as far as possible, avoid doing things that are not important.

We all know that one day we will die. It's one of the few things that we know for sure, at least that this body and mind as we know them will disintegrate. We know it, but we prefer not to think about it. We avoid the thought of death, and, when it does pop up and become more intrusive – maybe when someone close to us dies, a parent, a partner, or another important person in our life – we feel uncomfortable.

The downside of trying to keep the knowledge of death at bay is that it prevents us from living fully, here and now, and making the most of our time on Earth.

We can live more wholeheartedly and fully if we allow the idea of death to be present in our lives. We don't need to go overboard thinking about death all the time. But, when the awareness comes up, we can treat it like an old friend who reminds us: 'Of course, my life doesn't last forever. Do I spend my time making plans for the future that don't take death into account? Let me instead seize this moment, because it is the only one I can truly say that I have.'

Our actions have consequences – karma

Karma is a complex concept, but the word really just means 'action'. In this context, it is enough to understand how our conscious actions and the choices we make in life affect how we experience our life. This is not an ironclad law, but rather a fairly general wisdom of life. This wisdom lives on in many of our common proverbs: 'As you make your bed, so you must lie in it', 'You reap what you sow', and 'What goes around comes around.'

As we are social beings, it is quite natural that there is a connection between how we treat others and how we ourselves are treated. The problem is that life has become so complex that we are not always aware of this relationship, and that we therefore can begin to doubt that there is any relationship at all.

We often feel that adversity and misfortune are unfair, that we don't deserve them. We easily forget that justice isn't something inherent in the universe, but something that we humans have to create ourselves. Sometimes we aren't so good at it, and sometimes we do better.

In general, however, if we are generous and kind, others are more likely to treat us in the same way. It is also the case that generosity and kindness carry their own reward, in that it is much more pleasant to be filled with such feelings than with greed and ill will.

The unsatisfactory nature of cyclical existence

The necessary foundations for lojong also include the realization that life is inherently unsatisfactory. We have already noted that life is not fair. It is also fragile, and can be interrupted at any time by illness and death.

Whatever we choose to do with our life, it will also have its clear limitations. For all the things we choose – profession, partner, lifestyle, interests, or beliefs – there are an infinite number of things we simultaneously choose not to do. We will never know if something else would have been better than what we chose.

Preparations

And, whatever we choose, there will always be some elements that we find unsatisfactory. In some areas we do have choice. For example, we can change jobs or partners. There are other things we cannot opt out of, for instance if we have brought children into the world.

Often the best we can do is to work with what has become our life and make the most of it. This means accepting that life is not entirely satisfying and can never be.

Reflection

This unique opportunity

Sit quietly for a while, and just land in yourself. Feel your body and the contact with what you are sitting on, feel your breathing and allow it room within you. You can sit with your eyes open at first and then close them if you feel like it or continue to sit with your eyes open. Keeping your eyes open may create more clarity – this varies between individuals, so try it out. Just be open to your experience as it is right now, including thoughts that come and go, without being consumed by them.

Then reflect on the fact that you have a body, a mind, and an intellect that is functioning reasonably well; you have come into contact with the Dharma and this teaching. You are aware – how marvellous is that! You live in a country and at a time when you have access to so much teaching. But are you using this opportunity? Do you value it? You can ask yourself: 'What am I doing with my life?', 'What do I really want to do?', and 'What is important to me?'

Sit with these questions for a while, and notice the answers and thoughts that emerge. Later, you may want to write them down in a reflection book and reflect upon them further.

Many teachers have written their own verses about 'the reminders'. Here is a short verse on one of the reminders, the transience of life:

> This threefold world is as fleeting as an autumn cloud.
> Living beings are born and die like actors on a stage.
> The length of my life rushes by like a torrent down a steep mountain.
> My life will one day quickly and abruptly come to an end,
> like a bolt of lightning in the sky.[8]

Exercise

Ground yourself in your experience

Here is a meditation on the dissatisfaction of life and on karma. How do you relate to suffering and dissatisfaction (dukkha), which of course is an inevitable part of life?

Buddhism often emphasizes that we cannot change the basic conditions – we get sick, we lose things or a partner, things go wrong – but we can change our attitude to

Preparations

what is happening. The problem, therefore, is not that it happens, but that we don't want to see or face it; rather we often tend to turn away and seek sensual pleasures or distractions.

It is therefore good to practise being with your experience – just as it is and with a friendly awareness. As you sit here reading, take a few deeper breaths and feel what you are sitting on. Feel the contact between your buttocks and the chair and notice your hands holding the book (mobile phone or tablet). Then feel your breath coming and going, and relax. Notice your surroundings and the sounds that are present. How does it feel to sit here? Are you calm and comfortable, or anxious and restless, or something else? Allow yourself to rest within yourself for a moment.

Point Two

Absolute and Relative Bodhicitta

When we have achieved a certain psychological stability, in other words when we have developed into well-integrated individuals with a reasonably positive self-esteem and understanding of what is important in life, we are in a position to open ourselves to deeper aspects of life.

The preparation needed to move on to the other points may include psychological work to address personal difficulties that may hinder the development of compassion. It also requires basic training in mindfulness and meditation practices, such as mindfulness of breathing and the cultivation of loving-kindness.[9]

Once we have built up a solid foundation of mindful awareness and emotional positivity, we can begin to open up to the mysteries of life. In Buddhism, the mysteries of life are expressed in realizations such as non-self and the emptiness of all ideas and concepts whatsoever. Concepts such as non-self and emptiness are not beliefs that we are expected to accept or reject. Rather, they are perspectives that we are invited to explore in our own experience.

As we have seen, the overall aim of lojong is to develop wisdom and compassion in the sense of bodhicitta. Absolute bodhicitta means seeing the emptiness of all phenomena, including such things as suffering and living beings. But it does not mean a cold and unemotional view. Absolute bodhicitta is characterized by love and care.

Relative bodhicitta means a loving and compassionate response to other living beings in concrete situations where we are also confronted with suffering. It is impossible to love without at the same time being confronted with suffering. Relative compassion is therefore also about dealing with suffering when we encounter it.

The distinction between absolute bodhicitta and relative bodhicitta is not sharp. On the one hand, absolute bodhicitta must be expressed through relative bodhicitta in direct interaction with other people in order for it to be real. Relative bodhicitta, on the other hand, must be rooted in absolute bodhicitta in order for us to respond to suffering in a wise and constructive way. Sometimes, as in meditation, absolute bodhicitta may come to the fore. At other times, when we are confronted with difficult situations and encounter pain, suffering, and death, relative bodhicitta comes to the fore.

Absolute Bodhicitta

Slogans two to six are essentially about how we develop absolute bodhicitta. Here we jump straight in at the deep end. One might wonder why the creators of lojong chose to start with what is most difficult to understand. The idea can't have been that we at the start must grasp the full meaning of the deep insights that are presented. It is enough that we get a general sense of what absolute bodhicitta is. As we practise the more concrete and easily understood parts of lojong, we will over time gain a deeper understanding of the insights that underlie the whole practice.

Absolute and Relative Bodhicitta

Slogan Two: Think of Things as Dreamlike

According to physics, the universe is made up of different types of elementary particles, such as quarks, leptons, and bosons, and four fundamental forces: gravity, the strong nuclear force, the weak nuclear force, and electromagnetism. The elementary particles can also be seen as waves and, according to string theory, the smallest components of existence are one-dimensional vibrating strings.

Besides these elementary particles, or wave motions, or vibrating strings, interacting through the forces of nature, there is another dimension: consciousness. Scientists do not know whether consciousness is something separate from the known components of our physical universe, or whether it consists of, or is even identical to, them.

In fact, there is only one thing we can be really sure of: we are conscious, and we have experiences. We can doubt *what* we are experiencing, but we cannot doubt *that* we are experiencing.

Through evolution, humans have developed the ability to recognize patterns in their experience. There has undoubtedly been a survival value to perceiving these patterns, and to reacting with different emotions – like fear, love, anger, or curiosity – to what we perceive.

The problem is that our pattern recognition is quite arbitrary. Different individuals recognize different patterns, and the same individual can recognize different patterns depending on the context and the prevailing mood.

Dreams give us an indication of how fluid and indeterminate our perception of reality really is. By practising looking at our waking life in the same way we look at our dreams, we free ourselves from the naive realism that tends to make us rigid and literal-minded and thus easily fall victim to our emotional reactions to what we imagine.

Among the patterns we seem to recognize, there is one that causes us particular concern. It is the notion of a self that has certain characteristics and that constitutes a continuum from birth to death. We imagine that this self needs to possess more and more things – toys, clothes, a car, a house – in order to feel secure, which then solidifies the sense of a self. The reputation and social status of the self need to be maintained and, if someone or something threatens the self's material or immaterial assets, we think we must defend it. This idea of an isolated and continuous self gives rise to stress, fear, hatred, envy, and a whole range of other emotions that plague us.

If we can see that our so-called self consists only of thoughts and stories created by ourselves or others, it loses much of its power to generate all those emotions and the drama that those emotions give rise to. Instead, we see that the self is also dreamlike. It emerges as an illusion when we interact with others, but dissolves and reshapes itself anew depending on the context.

The slogan tells us to consider our waking experience as *dreamlike*, not that it literally *is* a dream. It is a method, rather than a statement of fact. The slogan provides an antidote, a remedy, to our tendency to see our experience of reality as absolutely true and unshakeable. We can learn to recognize that our thoughts are just thoughts – not absolute truths. Of course, we can be right in the way we think, but we can also be wrong.

Exercise

 Do you add a story?

In this exercise, you become aware of suffering – that of others and your own – and notice what you do with the experience.

First, sit for a little while and ground yourself in your body and breathing. Then think of a person who you know is struggling or suffering (or, if you prefer, think of something painful in your own life). Try to feel and empathize with how the person might be feeling, what it is that is difficult. Can you meet this suffering as it is, or do you add a story, an explanation, or a comment? Just note kindly and patiently. Come back to your body and your breathing, and then return to the person, their pain or yours. Can you stay there, breathing with it? You don't have to do anything about the problem or come up with a solution.

Although we all experience suffering and difficulties, they are not fixed and unchangeable. They have arisen due to conditions and, if these conditions change or cease, the suffering also ceases or changes. If you notice that you are adding a story, you can also not do so. You can choose to stay with what is, coming back to your actual experience – your body and breathing. Notice the tendency to escape, perhaps to a pleasant fantasy.

A buddha or bodhisattva does not make up stories. They meet experiences and people as they are – they

see the suffering, they see the person, but they also
see the conditioned nature of it and the possibility of
change.

Slogan Three: Explore the Nature of Unborn Awareness

When we meditate, we eventually discover that all experiences have the same basic nature. They arise, last for a short time, and then disappear. There is no fundamental difference between what we call 'outer' and 'inner'. Things we experience with our senses – with sight, hearing, taste, smell, and touch – have the same character, whether we can classify them as 'external' or 'internal', if they are outside or inside our body. The same applies to thoughts, which are made up of words and images, in other words auditory and visual impressions.

To give an example: we sit in a park and suddenly hear a bird singing. The sound arises from silence, and after a while all is quiet again. Where is the sound? Does it come from the trees nearby or is it in our ears, or our head?

Instead of the usual division into inner and outer, we can become more and more aware of two other poles of our experience: the phenomena we experience, and the experience itself – the experience as a witness to everything that happens.

We can continue to explore this pure form of awareness, which observes all phenomena, but is itself devoid of form and content. In Tibetan Buddhism it is often said to be characterized by emptiness and luminosity. It has no content but is at the same time luminous and clear.

This luminous emptiness is the 'unborn awareness', unborn because it has not taken concrete form but exists only as potential. Because it is unborn, it cannot die. It does not age. It cannot be destroyed, tainted, or distorted. All contents of consciousness, all experiences, are constantly changing, but the *knowing* itself remains constant.

Exercise

 The nature of awareness: openness, clarity, and sensitivity

A traditional way to explore the nature of awareness is to become aware of its three inherent qualities. By becoming aware of these qualities, they grow and emerge more clearly. The first quality is *openness*. Awareness does not have a specific place in space, it is intangible and therefore completely open. Examine this openness. For example, you can be open to all the experiences you have, all the sensations and impressions that arise and flow in through your sense organs. Notice how it feels to be open in this way, open, for example, to all sounds. Stop and just listen. Can you be open and receptive to all sounds? What effect does this have on your body?

The second quality is *clarity*. When you become aware of something, say the sight of a flower, a person in front of you, or a striking colour or shape in your vicinity, you find that it becomes clearer, brighter, in the light of awareness. There is a clear knowing – this is my experience. Touch this clarity, feel it within you, notice its quality in your mind and heart. It's like when you have been to a rewarding art exhibition or a moving performance, and then leave the place and go out. Then everything you see can seem so clear and distinct. I experienced this strongly once when I came out onto Trafalgar Square in London, after walking around the National Gallery and looking at the colourful and beautiful paintings there. Everything in the cityscape down towards Big Ben shimmered and stood out clearly.

The third and final quality is *sensitivity*, which is the responsive, emotional side of awareness. You can also think of it as warmth or kindness or even love – try it out and see how you experience it. As you sit here reading, take a moment to listen inwardly and feel your inner experience, rest your attention in your heart, in your centre, and see if you can find a warmth there, a gentle care, a kindness. What's it like to sit with this quality?

Like the other qualities, sensitivity is inherent. It is always there, but we can lose touch with it when we, for example, become stressed or too mentally preoccupied with our tasks or chores. Like the other qualities, it grows and becomes more apparent the more we pay attention to it and recognize it in our experience.

Sit for a while and play with these three qualities. Notice them in your body, in the experience of breathing, in your thoughts, and so on. You can always come back to these three qualities because they are always there, to some extent.

Slogan Four: Let Even the Antidote Free Itself

Buddhist concepts such as non-self and emptiness can be seen as antidotes or remedies. Their purpose is to counteract our deeply ingrained tendency to see our self and other things as more real – more solid, unchanging, and absolute – than they really are.

It is convenient to talk about a self. When we say something like 'I will buy milk on my way home from work today', it can be a meaningful statement. Similarly, if I say 'I was born in Lapland.' This can be valuable information in some situations, and perhaps it says something about me as a person.

But when we try to define the self more precisely, we discover that there is no entity, no function in the brain or elsewhere, that corresponds to the self. Reflecting on non-self is a method that seeks to loosen our naive notion of a fixed and unchanging self, thereby making us less attached to and preoccupied with that self.

But the antidote is only a means to achieving freedom from attachment to the self. We must also be able to let go of the idea of non-self so that it does not become a dogmatic notion. In a famous statement, the Buddha said that his entire teaching, the Dharma, is like a raft. With the raft you can cross the river of suffering. But, once you have reached the other bank, there is no need to hold on to the raft.

By seeing all phenomena as empty in their innermost nature, we can allow them to liberate themselves. That they self-liberate means that we don't have to do anything other than bring our awareness to them, in order to let the bonds and locks of our way of thinking dissolve. It is not something we can think our way to; we can only experience it in meditation and in direct experience.

Slogan Five: Rest in Alaya, the Fundamental Nature of All Experiences

Our life – our real life – consists of all conscious experiences. In the philosophical approach known as Yogacara, the basis of all these experiences is a layer of consciousness, or an aspect of consciousness, called 'alaya'. Everything we've thought and done in life – and even in previous lives – has left traces that influence and colour our experience of life. It's an idea that interestingly anticipates modern notions of the unconscious and the understanding of brain function provided by brain research today.[10]

Resting in alaya, the fundamental nature of all experience, means taking a relaxed approach to everything that happens and giving up the illusion that we are in control of life, as it unfolds. The illusion of control is linked to the idea of a fixed and unchanging self that, like a pilot, guides us through the various stages of life.

In fact, we fly mostly on autopilot and the 'pilot', which is our conscious experience, doesn't really have to do much more than enjoy the view, check the instruments, and make minor adjustments if necessary. It goes well anyway, in fact much better than if the pilot tried to control every single moment of the flight.

Every time we start to worry about not being in control and panic about what might happen, contemplating different scenarios and wondering how we could hypothetically act in such situations, we can try to sit back, become curious, and trust that things will work out.

This approach is also an antidote and not something we should take too literally and cling to. Of course, sometimes we need to think things through and then formulate a plan of action. But far too often our natural tendency is to worry unnecessarily.

What the slogan is trying to convey is that we should try not to resist and prevent the natural process by which the fruits of our past actions are expressed. Instead, we should relax and face all experiences with awareness and acceptance. To the extent that we experience the fruits of unhealthy thought patterns and actions, they will eventually run their course, and the dark shadows of the past will dissipate.

Exercise

 Just sit and do nothing

Sometimes, when we have lost something or can't remember where we put it, we may realize after a short or long time that it is right in front of us. The nature of consciousness is somewhat like that.

Train Your Mind

Certainly, our awareness grows and becomes clearer with practice and meditation, and as we try to be mindful in all our daily activities. But sometimes it seems to go under the radar, slipping out of our hands when we get distracted or engrossed in our emotions and thoughts.

The good news is that it is there after all, right in front of us or within us or everywhere – and has been there all along. If only we realized this deeply! Whether we have temporarily lost sight of it and want to get it back, or whether we want to strengthen it, there is one thing that in my experience is very effective – doing nothing.

What does that mean? How do you do nothing? This sounds like one of those Zen koans, an impossible thing. But it can be done. The best way is to simply sit down on a sofa or an armchair (or just stand, if you prefer). Don't try to meditate or be clever. Just sit there. Look out the window or straight ahead of you into the room or at what's in front of you. You see what's there, but you don't do anything with it. If thoughts arise, just observe them (kindly) and continue to sit. (Then the thoughts usually go away on their own, but not always.)

You sit like this for a while, and just relax and let go of the tendency to want to do something with the moment, to think about something or whatever.

When you sit there you become aware of your awareness, that you are sitting here, that you are breathing, but above all that you are here, present, aware. How does that feel? And relax!

Absolute and Relative Bodhicitta

You can sit like that (or stand) for five, ten, fifteen minutes, or half an hour if you feel like it, as long as it feels relaxed, natural, and rewarding. See if you can take the feeling from the exercise into the rest of your life. Occasionally, you can just stop and tune in with awareness – which is always there.

Slogan Six: Between Meditations, Play with the Illusions

When practising lojong, everything you do is practice. The practice can be divided into meditation and post-meditation. In post-meditation, we interact with the world and other people, and must necessarily relate to our own and others' illusions. The slogan tells us to be more like children and play with reality.

We may think that children play and that adults take life seriously. But is there really such a crucial difference between children's play and what adults do so 'seriously'? Isn't it just that adults define their own play as serious?

When we clearly see that all human interaction is based on illusions created by our pattern-recognizing brain, we also see that we are actually playing games.

At the same time, our games are serious in that suffering is tangible and real. When we create suffering for ourselves and others, we should learn to stop it and instead engage in games where we free ourselves and others from suffering.

Suppose that we have just come out of meditation, when we get a call from a young friend who tells us that she has just broken up with a partner. She is heartbroken and cries while telling us about it. Part of us is aware of the illusory nature of young love and the fact that our young friend will soon get over her heartache. But we listen to our friend with genuine care and concern, knowing that it will take time for her to get over her loss.

This slogan is about how we can learn to alternate between meditation and daily activities, between rest and movement, and between absolute and relative bodhicitta, with harmony and balance.

Relative Bodhicitta

Slogans seven to ten describe the basis of relative bodhicitta and how we can use meditation as a means to develop relative bodhicitta.

Slogan Seven: Practise Giving and Receiving Alternately. Place Them on the Breath

The seventh slogan refers to tonglen, the meditation practice that permeates the entire lojong practice. 'Tonglen' means 'giving and receiving'. Teachers give instructions for tonglen in slightly different ways, but basically the meditation involves breathing in suffering and sorrow, one's own and that of others, and breathing out relief from that suffering, peace, and happiness. If you wish, you can visualize the suffering as thick, sticky smoke that you breathe in and the relief you breathe out as a white light or a white, luminous mist.

Absolute and Relative Bodhicitta

It's a meditation that at first can seem strange, perhaps even frightening. It goes against all our instincts, to voluntarily breathe in suffering, even if it is something we only imagine that we are doing. What is important and crucial is what happens in our body when the suffering is transformed into soothing and healing energy that we then breathe out.

It is important to realize that it is not our own limited 'self' that transforms negative influences into positive ones. We need to feel that we are in touch with forces greater than ourselves, for instance the buddhas and bodhisattvas, the true nature of existence, the power of love and compassion, or other positive forces.

Tonglen challenges in a direct and immediate way our tendency to constantly secure the self and grasp at anything that supports it. We therefore need to recognize that attachment to the self is indeed the source of suffering, stress, and tension in our lives. If we can do that, we can also give ourselves to the practice – even though it may be demanding and uncomfortable at times – knowing that it serves as a remedy for the root cause of our difficulties and hardships.

We also need to recognize that we are not alone in our suffering. All beings, all of us, suffer because we do not realize how deeply rooted we all are in ego attachment and how, because of that, we continue to create the conditions for more suffering. This realization gives a strong focus to the practice and a sense of urgency to overcome our ego-creating tendencies, our 'selfing'.

As we inhale, we breathe in acceptance and receptivity. We open up to the suffering of ourselves and others. On the exhalation, we breathe out love and care. The fact that the breath carries the practice makes it easier not to get stuck in thoughts and beliefs.

It is important that, in this receiving and giving, we do not exclude our own suffering, including feelings of inadequacy or other experiences that may arise in the practice. It is by seeing and recognizing suffering and its causes in ourselves that we can also fully accept it in others.

All forms of life are subject to ageing, disease, and death. All living beings seek pleasure and happiness and try to escape suffering, from the smallest insect to us humans. This fact connects us experientially with all living beings. It also leads to a focus on the suffering as such, rather than on the 'owner' of the suffering. It does not matter so much whether it is 'my suffering' or 'suffering out there'.

Finally, it is important to visualize some kind of happy outcome of the exercise. We can do this by imagining how all the care, love, presence, and openness are received by ourselves and others, and how they lead to reduced suffering, and an increased sense of freedom and happiness.

Again, it is not that 'we' have done well and thereby made a difference, but rather that the power of bodhicitta manifests itself when we step aside and entrust the practice to that which is beyond the self. We focus not only on suffering but also on its cessation. So the practice is fundamentally joyful.

Slogan Eight: Three Types of Objects, Three Poisons, Three Seeds of Goodness

This slogan is about the way we automatically perceive and categorize our experiences and then relate to them in a certain way.

All our experiences are tinged with feeling tones, so that they are either pleasant, unpleasant, or neutral. These three feeling tones are automatic and inbuilt in our psychophysical organism, and based on them we react and behave in three different ways.

We usually want to own or have more of what we experience as pleasant. What we experience as unpleasant we want to avoid or get rid of. In the third category, we tend to be disinterested or indifferent about what we experience as neutral.

These three behaviours correspond to the three basic mental poisons: desire, ill will, and unawareness.[11]

These poisons can be seen as evolutionary driving forces that favoured our survival. In a state of constant scarcity of food and other resources, our tendency to accumulate resources has given our species an advantage. Similarly, our instinct to avoid anything unpleasant has had a protective effect against all the threats and dangers. Through disinterest in neutral things, which present neither benefits nor threats, we avoid wasting time on them unnecessarily.

But these instincts are not so helpful and functional today and in the circumstances that most of us reading this live in. When we have more than enough assets to ensure our survival, and when we are not constantly surrounded by threats to our existence, these same instincts often work against us. We don't feel satisfied with what we have, and constantly want more. At the same time, we perceive hostility and threats where there may not be anything to really fear. By being disinterested in things from which we can't imagine a direct benefit, or that don't seem to pose a direct threat to us, we miss out on many of life's opportunities.

This slogan invites us to reverse these reactive patterns. As with the tonglen meditation, we are asked not to automatically shy away from what we find unpleasant, but to face it with an open mind. We can enjoy what we find pleasant in the moment, while being prepared to let go of the pleasant experiences as they fade and disappear, as all experiences do. When it comes to neutral experiences, we are encouraged to be curious and examine them a little more closely. Perhaps there is more to them than we initially realize.

The practice is essentially about abandoning a *reactive* attitude to the world and developing a *creative* one.[12] When we are reactive, we follow a very limited repertoire of behavioural patterns. Our actions become predictable and stereotypical. When we are creative, we are aware of many more ways in which we can respond. Our experience of the world becomes much richer, and our ability to respond to different situations becomes more diverse and better adapted to reality.

People are also objects of experience, so this process ('the three types of objects') affects our relationships as well. We are attracted to people we like and want to associate with them, while we tend to avoid or push away the people we dislike. Those we neither like nor dislike tend to leave us indifferent and uninterested.

By being less reactive and more creative, we can continue to meet those we like, but now without the tendency to hold on to them or become dependent on them. Those we spontaneously dislike we can learn to meet and relate to in a more creative way, and thereby perhaps discover that we have more in common with them than we initially thought. In the case of neutral people, we can begin to take an interest in them and find out more about them.

With this approach, we discover that there is more that unites us than separates us. In this way, the three poisons are transformed into three seeds of goodness. Desire is transformed into the joy of encountering the pleasurable and contentment with what we have, resentment is transformed into acceptance and patience, unawareness and disinterest are transformed into awareness and understanding.

Slogan Nine: Practise Using Slogans in All Activities

The purpose of slogans is to make them easy to remember and therefore easy to recall when we need them, so they should have striking and slightly catchy wording. Some of them are self-explanatory; others need an explanation. The important thing is that you know what they mean and that you keep them alive by thinking about them from time to time.

You can choose one sentence per day to reflect on, either by going through them systematically in numerical order, or by selecting one or two at random. There are several collections of cards available for purchase, or you can write your own cards with slogans.

Lojong is put together in a clever way that covers many of life's situations. Once you understand the basic principles, you can, if you wish, create your own slogans based on the challenges you feel you have in your life.

Slogan Ten: Start Giving and Receiving with Yourself

As we saw earlier, it is important to include yourself, your own suffering and difficulties, when practising tonglen. One way to do this is to visualize sitting in front of yourself while meditating. You see yourself as one being among others: you have your own difficulties and suffering, but you also have the potential to feel love and compassion, peace and happiness. You breathe in sorrow and pain, and you breathe out well-being and healing.

By visualizing ourselves in this way, we clarify that we can be both the experiencer of suffering and the giver of love and care. We are all in the same boat: we add to our suffering with our self-centredness and attachment to 'I', 'me', and 'mine'.

What we do in tonglen is to surrender ourselves and all other suffering selves to a force that works through us and others, a force for good in the world. As a Buddhist, one can think of this force as the buddhas and bodhisattvas, or we can perceive love and compassion as a force expressing itself in human actions.

Meditation

Tonglen

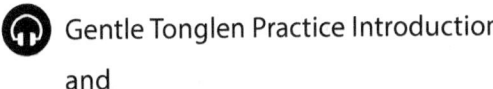 Gentle Tonglen Practice Introduction

and

 Tonglen Full Practice

Start by just sitting for a while and relaxing. It is important that you give yourself this time to just be. Then feel your body and the contact with what you are sitting on and relax. Feel your breath, inhaling and exhaling, and notice where you feel the breath in your body. If you want, take a few deeper breaths and relax even more. Then sit for a while with the breath and all the sensations in your body.

It is often helpful to think that you are doing this meditation with others – your spiritual teachers and role models or the Buddha, perhaps a specific buddha you feel attracted to. Think of them doing the practice with you, and their compassion and wisdom flowing down to you and through you. Come back to this image from time to time in the meditation.

After a while, you can bring your attention to your chest and stomach, and notice how you feel. Allow space for all feelings and experiences: everything is okay. If you feel tension or pain somewhere, breathe with that, into the tense area, into the pain or feeling. As you breathe out, you may think or imagine that the area softens and fills with warmth, light, and relief. But it may also be that the relief comes on the inhalation. Notice what happens in your experience and what is helpful. Then sit for a while with the breath, and be aware of any pain and suffering you experience (sometimes it is quite a subtle thing) and how it is relieved, dissolved, and transformed by the breath.

Then think of a person – perhaps a friend or loved one – who you know is struggling, ill, or suffering in some way. Become aware of the person and their difficulty or suffering. Breathe with it. Remember that you are not alone in doing this. Imagine breathing in the pain and suffering (perhaps as a shadow or smoke), and breathing out relief, light, and healing. You don't have to synchronize the breathing with this. For a while you can focus on breathing with the suffering, then for a while on relief and light, and so on. Calmly come back to your body and how it feels right now. Relax and feel the connection with love, warmth, and compassion – which are both within you and in others.

Now you can choose to think of another person who is having a hard time, or you can expand to several people, perhaps an area of the world where you know there is a lot of suffering right now. Breathe with the weight, the pain you know is there, and at the same time bring in light, relief, warmth, and care. There is suffering and difficulty everywhere in the world – everyone has their share – and it will always be so. Suffering and pain are an inevitable part of life, of everybody's life. At the end, you can sit with this broader knowledge and breathe calmly. Imagine the suffering being transformed into relief, light, and warmth.

Absolute and Relative Bodhicitta

Then finish the meditation by just sitting for a while and relaxing. Notice how it feels inside you, and feel free to take some aspect of this exercise with you when you leave and face the world. When you become aware of suffering and difficulties around you, you can see and feel this, and breathe with it.

Point Three

Turning Difficulties into Means of Awakening

With point three, we come to the core of the lojong teachings. Practising under favourable circumstances and developing peaceful and pleasant states of mind is all well and good. But what do we do if the circumstances are not so favourable? Atisha puts it in a few pithy slogans:

> Difficulties are your spiritual friend. Suffering is a gift that nature gives us. Bad omens are good news.

During periods in which I have experienced difficulties myself, I have drawn strength and inspiration from Atisha's attitude expressed in these three sentences. We don't need to seek out suffering and difficulties – sooner or later they will find us anyway. But it will be much easier to cope with them if, instead of trying to hide and run away, we calmly stand our ground and say: let it come!

Slogans eleven to sixteen are about how we can practise when we face different kinds of difficulties.

Slogan Eleven: When the World Is Filled with Evil, Transform All Unfavourable Conditions into Means of Awakening

Sooner or later, we will all face difficulties such as illness, suffering, and death, for ourselves or our loved ones.

Sometimes we also encounter harm, when people deliberately cause us or others suffering.

The aim of the practice is to be able to use even such situations as a means of awakening. To do so, we must accept that grief and pain are natural parts of life. Even human cruelty is part of life, however much we wish it were not.

Accepting suffering and cruelty does not mean that we refrain from doing what we can to prevent it. It just means that we recognize it is a fact of life. If thoughts pop up like: 'This can't be true, why me?', 'This is so unfair', 'I refuse to accept this', we can examine them more closely and ask ourselves: 'Why not? It happens to others, so why not to me?'

When we feel that others are causing us pain, it can trigger thoughts of retaliation and revenge. However, if we examine such thoughts a little more closely, we realize that revenge is rather pointless. The idea that one should retaliate – 'an eye for an eye, a tooth for a tooth' – and cause suffering to the offender, as a kind of compensation for the suffering one has suffered, is really absurd.

The idea of revenge means that we harbour a belief that there is an imbalance that needs to be redressed. But, if we try to equalize the situation by harming the offender, it only means that we lower ourselves to the same base moral ground. We do ourselves a greater favour if we preserve our dignity, and instead act in a way that encourages the offender to rise to a higher level. It can be important to confront the offender with what we feel he or she has done. But then we must also be prepared to hear their version and be open to the possibility that we may have made a mistake. Perhaps there was no malicious intent behind the act that caused us suffering.

However, it may of course be a real perpetrator with a desire to harm, or at least with indifference to our or others' suffering. We can then clearly express that this is not a behaviour we accept, and that we will do what we can to prevent it from happening again.

Depending on the seriousness of the offence, there may be grounds for some form of accountability or sanction. If it is a criminal offence, we should report it to the police.

Once we have done what needs to be done, the challenge is to move on. If we have acted in a way that upholds our dignity and, to the extent possible, prevents further harm to oneself or others, we don't need to feel any shame or guilt ourselves. We may even feel grateful for the opportunity to strengthen our integrity and morality. It is relatively easy to show love and compassion when we are surrounded by kind people. It is much more difficult to do so in the presence of wickedness and malice. This is why the old masters say that we should consider enemies as our benefactors. They help us make progress on the path, sometimes much more effectively than our friends can.

Living according to this slogan is certainly easier said than done. But that's what lojong is all about: uncompromisingly attacking deep-seated tendencies until we eventually learn to live more in tune with a deeper reality.

Slogan Twelve: Blame It All on the One Culprit

All subjective and unnecessary suffering is due to one thing: our attachment to the self. When we start looking in our minds for someone to blame for the discomfort or suffering that we experience, that is a symptom of our egocentricity. What the slogan is saying is that, at that point, we should break the pattern and instead see that all suffering is caused by our self-centredness. If we hadn't been so self-absorbed to begin with, we wouldn't have started thinking about who to blame.

Let's take a simple example. Imagine someone pushing in front of you as you drive. Your first impulse may be irritation, thinking that the person is being selfish. But what if they have a passenger who is ill, and they are in a hurry to get to the hospital?

Instead of looking for someone to blame, and by extension perhaps someone to punish, we could learn to look for the causes and conditions that have given rise to the suffering or discomfort.

Blaming others or blaming ourselves is never helpful. Many things can cause pain, but the concept of blame is only relevant when we imagine that a 'you' is causing pain to an 'I'. If we clearly see that 'you' and 'I' are notions that only exist in a relative sense, we realize that there is really only one thing we can rightly blame for all suffering, namely the very notion of a 'you' and an 'I' in an absolute sense and a clinging to that.

Slogan Thirteen: Be Grateful to Everyone

This slogan does not mean adopting a submissive position in social contexts. Expressing gratitude because of fear or a sense of inferiority is false gratitude.

Turning Difficulties into Means of Awakening

What the slogan refers to is a gratitude that we can learn from all new experiences. Ultimately, it is gratitude to life, gratitude for being born as an aware being, with a body and a mind.

Our wealth is measured not by the number of possessions we have but by the amount of gratitude we feel. And gratitude can be practised, just like any other emotion. 'What can I be grateful about today?' we may ask ourselves. 'Everything!' is the answer to this slogan.

We also have reason to be grateful to those who criticize us. If we feel offended and hurt by their criticisms, they help us to see where we are still bound to an illusory self. Anyone who clearly sees through the self cannot be hurt by criticism. On the contrary, all criticism is valuable help. It is all information for us. Even if we don't think there is much to the criticism, we learn that there is at least one person – the critic – who thinks that we have done wrong.

Tibetan Buddhists have a mind game called 'nose or horn', which they use as an antidote to angry reactions to criticism. If we leave aside things like the tone of voice or the anger behind the criticism, is what we are being criticized for true or not?

If it's true, it is as if the person is saying that we have a nose on our face. We both know it's true, so there's nothing to argue about. If we have done something wrong, we just admit to it and seek to do better.

If it's not true, it is as if the person is saying that we have a horn on our forehead. We know it's not true, so we don't need to get worked up about it: we can just calmly state that it's not true.

Exercise

Gratitude

A grateful life is a happy life; a happy life is a grateful life. If you make it a habit to recall and remember what you feel grateful for, you will find that it has an effect. It changes your state of mind, and it trains you to see and take notice of all the good things you have in your life. You can therefore, if you wish, think of three things that you feel grateful for, right now, and maybe write them down. Just sit here and dwell on these three things for a while. You can also do this at the end of the day, before you go to bed, so that you enter the sleeping state in a grateful mood.

Here are a few examples that I feel grateful for: my parents (although that can be a bit complex for some people; they gave me life and they cared for me in so many ways), my teachers (especially my Buddhist teachers, without whom I'd be lost), and my precious friends. I can easily choose a number of people who contribute to society working and running smoothly (garbage collectors, shop assistants, bus drivers, mechanics, builders, and many more). I'm also grateful to live in a house and environment I really appreciate, to have access to a computer that works, to have a bicycle. There is so much to be grateful for!

Turning Difficulties into Means of Awakening

Slogan Fourteen: Seeing Both Confusion and Awakening as Emptiness Is the Ultimate Protection

This slogan requires some explanation. The classic Tibetan commentary equates confusion with the Buddha's four bodies, *kayas*, a metaphysical division of the awakened mind into four aspects.[13] But the basic meaning of the slogan is that there is ultimately no difference between our confused mind and the awakened mind.

When we are confronted with our own or others' suffering, be it illness, pain, or death, our first reaction is often confusion. We don't know what to do; we may struggle to even comprehend what is happening. Eventually the picture gets clearer, and we become aware of our feelings, which may be fear, sadness, compassion, or just a quiet presence. We act in a way that feels appropriate to the situation.

The first moment of confusion and incomprehension is natural. We can learn to rest in the uncertainty and wait for the response that eventually comes, which is also natural. The slogan tells us that this process – our initial confusion, which changes into an interpretation and understanding of the situation that in turn enable action – is no different from how the awakened mind functions.

Awakening is the ability to see that our waking reality is like a dream, and that even our emotional reactions are illusory and transitory. They appear out of nowhere and disappear just as easily, turning into something else. Ultimately, there is no difference between the awakened mind and the ordinary mind.

The underlying idea of lojong is that the only thing that can harm us is our own mind when it is the victim of confusing illusions that give rise to fear, attachment, or aversion. When we see that the only thing that really exists is the awakened mind – and that it includes our confusion and illusions – there is nothing left to harm us anymore. In this way, realizing that confusion and awakening are both of the nature of emptiness is the ultimate protection.

Slogan Fifteen: Do Good, Purify Your Mind, Make Peace with the Demons, and Ask for Help

This slogan describes four approaches that we can use to tackle the inevitable difficulties we face in life, the second of which suggests using four powers.

Doing good is simply about being a good person: a good parent, a good colleague, a good friend, a responsible citizen, the kind of person we would like to meet in different situations in life. Buddhism talks about accumulating merit through skilful actions. The idea is that good actions build up an inner wealth of positive emotions that provide a solid foundation for further development.

The second approach is to cleanse or purify our mind of what is harmful and unhealthy. This refers to bad habits that we have developed, but also the mental traces that may remain as a result of unskilful actions committed earlier in life. For example, if we betrayed close friends or relatives, or perhaps even committed a serious crime, the memory of what we did will haunt us and hamper our attempts to develop positive states such as mindfulness and compassion.

Turning Difficulties into Means of Awakening

Sometimes betrayal of a loved one isn't obvious. We may simply feel that we have drifted away from someone who was once close to us, and that we no longer reach out to each other. This happened for me with my father for a number of years. I eventually realized that my betrayal was that I was not trying hard enough to resolve some of the issues we had with each other. Once I plucked up the courage to do so, our relationship changed radically for the better. I am now very grateful that I was able to do so before he became ill with dementia.

We can purify our minds with the help of four powers described in lojong. The first power is remorse, which means fully accepting that we have done wrong, without any excuses. Ideally, such remorse should be expressed to others, especially to those we have wronged. There is tremendous power in genuine and sincere repentance, and the result can often be liberating, both for oneself and for those who may have been affected.

But, at the same time, remorse must be accompanied by a determination not to do the same thing again. If the affected party does not feel that the remorse is accompanied by a determination not to repeat the action and a commitment to change behaviour, it is difficult to forgive. And, even if the nature of the act is such that there is nobody else affected and we have hurt only ourselves, the same thing applies. We can feel the hurt and take ourselves more seriously, and develop the motivation and action to change in order to forgive ourselves.

Sometimes remorse and determination are not enough in order for us to move forward. We may have committed serious actions, or the unhealthy habits are so ingrained that we cannot break them. In that case we need to ask for help. We can ask another person for help, or we can turn to the buddhas and bodhisattvas, the power of love in the universe, or whatever feels most natural to us. Sometimes it is enough to recognize that we cannot cope with the situation on our own and that we need help.

Finally, we can also apply the fourth power, atonement. For example, if we have stolen or otherwise acquired money dishonestly, we can make up for it by giving it away to others in need, if we cannot give it back to those we have taken it from.

The third approach that the slogan refers to is keeping peace with our demons. The original slogan in Tibetan talks about making offerings to *döns*, which are a kind of disease-causing spirits, but we can loosely translate *döns* as demons. Originally, the word 'demon' was used in the West to refer to spirit beings that cause illness, madness, and other harm. It also has a transferred psychological meaning, referring to certain characteristics and behaviours that we cannot control with our will. Demons in this sense can be seen as aspects of ourselves that sometimes take over in us, and they can be both destructive and chaotic.[14]

The Buddhist approach to such phenomena as demons is to try to make peace with them rather than to exorcize or destroy them. Instead of going to war with our inner demons, we can try to have a more relaxed and curious attitude towards them. We can look at our quirks with humour, and laugh at ourselves and how we sometimes behave. We can try to give our demons something of what they want, without compromising on our ethics. If we make friends with our demons, they will be much easier to deal with, and one day they will leave, when they feel they have nothing more to gain. Demons thrive on battle and conflict, and, if they don't face any resistance, they tend to lose interest.

The fourth and last approach is that when we face difficulties we need to ask for help. Firstly, we can ask for help from a good friend, someone who knows us well and shares our values: they understand our situation and can act as a Dharma friend.

In some situations this may not be enough, and we may need to ask for help from something greater than our conscious self. What is mentioned in lojong is that we can make offerings to *Dharmapalas*, the protectors of the Dharma. *Dharmapalas* are often depicted in Buddhist art as terrifying monsters, with sharp claws and fangs, surrounded by an aura of dazzling flames. But, unlike demons, they have our best interests at heart. Their way of counselling us and bringing us back to the right path when we're lost can be quite blunt, however. You could compare them to guardian spirits or the *fylgjas*[15] in Norse mythology.

Dharmapalas represent the invisible forces that shake us up and wake us up when we have lost our mindfulness and moral compass. Making offerings to them is a way of showing appreciation, and asking them to continue to watch over us and intervene when we run the risk of getting so lost that we may never find our way back.

When we ask for help, we need to ask for the right things. If we only ask for help to strengthen and protect the ego, it is not helpful. Jamgön Kongtrül emphasizes that we should primarily use prayer to end hope and fear:

If it is better for me to be sick,
I ask for the blessing of the disease.
If it is better for me to recover,
I ask for the blessing of recovery.
If it is better for me to die,
I pray for the blessing of death.[16]

This is a powerful prayer for critical situations where we can no longer influence the outcome, such as a serious illness. We have done what we can to get well. The best we can do now is to free ourselves from hope and fear, and face whatever happens with a calm and open mind.

Slogan Sixteen: Whenever You Encounter Something Unexpected, Combine It with Meditation

Life is full of unexpected events, both desirable and undesirable. Often, we are so surprised by the unexpected that we forget all our usual good intentions and get carried away. It could be something seemingly desirable like a crush or inheriting money. Or it could be something undesirable like an illness, the death of a loved one, an accident, or a natural disaster.

Whatever happens, we are invited here to meditate on the event, to give it time and space to sink in so that we can gain a better perspective. If we have a daily meditation practice, it is important that we stick to it and not get lured into frenetic activity by the new conditions that have arisen. In this way, we will not be tempted to act hastily and lose our good judgement.

Turning Difficulties into Means of Awakening

Meditation

The Bodhisattva of compassion and *om mani padme hum*

Bodhicitta is central to the whole lojong practice. At the beginning of the book, you read about the relative and absolute dimensions of bodhicitta. You could say that bodhicitta is a deep and unfathomable sense of care that everyone should be well, that everyone should grow and flourish, that they should ultimately be free and liberated from suffering. This is a really big ask, and it can be quite elusive. In the Buddhist tradition, a variety of practices and symbols, even figures, emerged that were imbued with and embodied the qualities of bodhicitta. One of the most important of these is the bodhisattva of compassion, Avalokiteshvara, 'the one who looks down on a suffering world with compassion' (Figure 1). His mantra – perhaps the most common of all mantras – is *om mani padme hum*. Figure 2 depicts the syllables of the mantra clockwise from twelve o'clock: *om, ma, ni, pa, dme,* and *hum*, with *hrih* at the centre, which is sometimes translated as 'self-respect'. By bringing this figure to mind and reciting this mantra, you tap into the qualities of compassion and let them become part of you. You can recite the mantra calmly and rhythmically for a while: *om mani padme hum, om mani padme hum...* and let your mind and heart be stilled. One interpretation of the word 'mantra' is 'that which protects the mind' and this is true, because, when you recite a mantra, you are thinking and doing something positive, thus protecting yourself from negative and unskilful mental states.

When Avalokiteshvara came to China and then to Japan, the bodhisattva took on a female form. Her name is Kuan Yin in Chinese and Kwannon in Japanese. There are many beautiful statues and images of these scattered around the world.

Figure 1 *Avalokiteshvara*

Turning Difficulties into Means of Awakening

Figure 2 *The mantra* om mani padme hum *in Tibetan*

Meditation

 Five Minute Breathing Break

You don't have to meditate for a long time to make a difference. Sometimes a period of five, ten, or fifteen minutes is enough, or just a short breathing break every now and then. Especially when you get into the habit of meditation, you can just stop between activities, take a few breaths, remind yourself of space and openness, or of kindness. Here are suggestions for a short five-minute meditation.

Sit down somewhere quiet or remote – or just wherever you are. Take a moment to just sit with your eyes open and feel the connection with what you are sitting on, the weight of your body and your feet on the ground or floor. And then feel your breathing. The body and the breath are always here, inviting you into the present and into awareness – when you are ready and when you allow them to. Take in what surrounds you, without necessarily looking around. Notice the colours and shapes, all the sounds, and even the silence between the sounds. Let the sounds just be there. Then come back to your body and breathing, take a few deeper breaths, and let go on the exhale. Just sit here and feel your breathing, inhalation and exhalation, and all the sensations in your body.

Then allow yourself to become aware of whatever thoughts and feelings are there, without having to latch on to them. It's more like taking a step back from your thoughts, more like *having* thoughts, rather than *being* your thoughts or feelings. If you still get lost in inner images or worries, just calmly come back to your body and breathing. Let your awareness come down to your hands, which may be in your lap. Rest your attention in your hands for a moment and let them relax, while you feel the breath coming and going. Sit like this for a while and enjoy being present, here and in your experience. Towards the end, let go of all effort, all striving, and just sit here, naturally and present. See if you can bring this feeling to the next activity, at least for a while, until you can take another break.

Point Four

Synthesis: Practice for a Whole Life

Point four summarizes the characteristics needed to live a good and meaningful life. We all thrive when we feel that our lives have a greater purpose and that we have the opportunity to use our abilities in a meaningful way.

If we feel that there is meaning and purpose in our life, we will also be able to face death with more equanimity and confidence. The two slogans under point four therefore address the same issues from two perspectives: how to live and how to die.

Slogan Seventeen: Make the Most of Your Life: Practise the Five Strengths

The five strengths are different qualities that we need in order to practise the Dharma effectively and to live a good and rich life. They are: *a heartfelt wish, familiarity, planting seeds of goodness, exposure,* and *transference of merit.*

Firstly, we need to find a goal for our life, something we feel is worth working and striving for – *a heartfelt wish*. We need some kind of vision of how we would like to live and what kind of person we would like to be. This is where other people can act as role models for us. Most of us probably feel intuitively that a life dedicated solely to promoting our own material interests is a limited and pointless life. We feel that we want to do something for others, and we hope that our life will contribute in some way to making the world a better place. The central ideal of Mahayana Buddhism is the Bodhisattva Ideal, which means dedicating one's life to promoting enlightenment and happiness for all beings.

The second strength we need to develop is *familiarity*. To realize our inner desire and vision, we need to remind ourselves time and again of what is important in life and to act on that. This is fundamentally about building good habits. By creating good habits inspired by our vision of a better life, we gradually begin to express our vision in thought, speech, and action. We make a habit of showing generosity, kindness, care, and concern for others. We make sure that we create space for meditation and reflection in our lives so that we can develop our awareness, compassion, and understanding.

This corresponds to what is known as the threefold path in Buddhism: ethics, meditation, and wisdom. These three aspects are mutually supportive. Effective meditation requires the foundation of a clear conscience and contentment that an ethical life can provide. And to gain wisdom through reflection requires concentration and awareness, which we can develop through meditation.

Thirdly, we need to *plant seeds of goodness*. We are all born with the capacity for love and compassion. Some branches of Mahayana Buddhism and Vajrayana speak of buddha nature as being inherent in everyone. With a modern scientific approach, the same idea can be expressed in terms of evolutionary biology: evolution has not only created us as selfish beings but also given us the ability to care for and

Synthesis: Practice for a Whole Life

nurture others. Initially, this applies to our children and members of our tribe, but the compassionate instinct can be developed to include more and more individuals and forms of life, until our compassion extends to all life. All-encompassing love and compassion are therefore not alien to our biological nature. On the contrary, the seeds are there, and all we need to do is to nourish those seeds so that they can grow. It is important to remember that we are talking about *seeds*. Seeds are small and barely noticeable. We do not need to think that we necessarily have to attract attention and 'make a difference' with the good seeds that we sow. Ideally, our seeds will do that in the long run, but first of all we need to learn to trust that sowing seeds is worthwhile, and to water and nourish them. In time, some of them at least will grow into fruiting plants.

The fourth strength we need to develop is the ability to *expose* what is unhealthy in our lives. We all have a tendency to hide our weaknesses and bad habits from others, but also a tendency to turn a blind eye to them or even deny them to ourselves. We need courage to expose ourselves to others but also to critically examine ourselves. This can be difficult to learn, a bit like lifting ourselves by the hair. But it is a habit we can develop. Once we have discovered the relief and joy of confessing our faults and shortcomings to others, or simply admitting to ourselves when we are ignorant or have acted thoughtlessly or selfishly, it becomes easier and easier over time.

The fifth strength is *transference of merit*. Merit in this context refers to the personal benefits we can gain from living a life with a clear vision, rooted in good habits, with the good seeds we have sown and the capacity for honesty and self-criticism. The idea is that we should share all these merits with all beings. For example, if we become popular with others and make many friends, if we are successful in our careers, we use these assets to help others. Merit in this sense is not a finite resource that diminishes when we entrust it to others. On the contrary, like love, it does not diminish but increases when we share it.

Traleg Kyabgon, commenting on the slogan, points out that we can use these five strengths in different ways in different situations. If we lack motivation, we can use our heartfelt wish as a strength. When we especially need stability in life, due to constantly fluctuating emotional states, we can use familiarity and establish good habits. When we need to break negative patterns, we can use exposure as a force to expose the negative patterns. By transferring our merits of these good actions, we amplify their effect and allow the good seeds to grow and develop even more.

Slogan Eighteen: Also Practise for the Moment of Death

Those who have developed the five strengths in their lives are also much better placed to face death as it approaches, with calm and confidence. Whatever ideas we have about death, and whether or not we believe in some kind of continuation of the stream of consciousness that we have been carrying, it will be easier to face death if we feel that we have lived life to the full and made the most of our time.

If we are able to consciously prepare ourselves as we approach the end of life, we should recall the five strengths. We

Synthesis: Practice for a Whole Life

can focus on a *heartfelt wish* that our life and work will benefit other living beings and that even our dying can be of help to others. If we imagine some kind of continuation after this life, we can express a wish that our stream of consciousness will continue to work for good in the world.

We can use the strength of *familiarity* by meditating, reciting mantras, or performing other rituals that connect us with what has been our practice throughout life.

We can see how, right up to the moment of death, we continue to *plant good seeds* that can grow and bear fruit, in future lives or in the hearts of others. By putting our affairs in order and making sure that our assets are distributed fairly among our descendants, we set an example for others and reduce the risk of disruptive inheritance disputes or painful conflicts among loved ones. This can also be a time to make gifts to various charities. Money and other material assets will no longer have any value to us, so there is no need to hold on to them until the end.

We can also use the *power of exposure* by confessing wrongs we may have committed against loved ones and trying to set things right as far as possible. Whilst we cannot undo things, we can try to heal emotional wounds and damaged relationships. As well as confessing our own wrongs, we may also need to forgive others around us, who either rightly or wrongly live under the impression that we hold a grudge against them because of past wrongs.

Finally, we can *transfer all our merits*, everything of value that we have created in our lives, for the benefit of all beings, and thereby create a powerful wish that will be carried forward in various ways when our physical existence ends.

We are then ready to let go not only of our possessions but also of our attachment to our bodies and our individual lives.

Whatever our thoughts on the possible continuation of life beyond death, a good death is in itself a noble thing to strive for. What the slogan is trying to say is that the secret of a good death is to first live a good life.

Reflection

Death

You can do this reflection when you are sitting as before or when you are walking around freely, without goals and time pressure. You might walk back and forth in an undisturbed place. When you feel grounded and in touch with yourself, you can reflect like this:

One day my life will come to an end. This is true for everyone. It is often said that there is not much we know for sure, but there is one thing we can be absolutely certain of: we will die. I don't know when or where or under what circumstances – but I will die.

What is my attitude towards death? Am I afraid of dying? Most people are, but what am I afraid of? Is it that everything will end, and I will lose everything I am attached to? Or am I afraid of something else around death, like losing control, or something bad happening afterwards?

Synthesis: Practice for a Whole Life

These are not easy questions, and we tend to habitually slide off them or latch on to something else. At least that's how it is for me. Notice if this happens and if you feel resistance to engaging with the issues, which is only natural.

According to traditional Buddhism, death is a transition from this life to the next – an end but also an opportunity. How do I see this myself? Is rebirth something I can embrace, or does it feel alien? Can I see death as an opportunity?

After reflecting on these questions for a while – ten or fifteen minutes, or longer if you are absorbed – you can take a break and do nothing before moving on to the next thing. Feel free to talk to your friends about how you think about death and these questions.

Point Five

Measuring the Effects of Our Practice

It is natural to want to have some kind of measure of progress in our training. But this is difficult for several reasons. First of all, it is difficult to measure qualities such as wisdom and compassion. How can we assess whether we have become wiser and more compassionate, and whether our lives are more characterized by wisdom and compassion? There are no measurable, objective criteria for such things. We have to rely on either our own judgement or that of others.

This brings us to the next difficulty. The judgement of others is of necessity based on outward signs of wisdom and compassion, and outward signs, as we all know, can be deceptive. Only we ourselves know what's going on inside us, in our thoughts and feelings. Unfortunately, we humans are not only good at deceiving others, but we are also good at deceiving ourselves. We can be gullible enough to tell others and ourselves that we are good and compassionate people, when the reality is quite different.

However, with practice and with the right kind of clues, we can be on our guard and learn to avoid deceiving ourselves. The following four slogans are intended to serve as such clues to help us determine if we are making progress, or if we need to work more on some aspect of our lives.

Slogan Nineteen: All Dharma Teaching Is Based on One Thing

If Dharma refers to the teachings of the Buddha, there is a rich variety of teachings, schools, and movements within what is commonly known as Buddhism. Buddhist literature is very extensive. The earliest writings preserved in the Pali Canon alone are eleven times the size of the Bible! The Mahayana sutras are even more extensive, and in addition there is secondary literature with commentaries on the scriptures written over two millennia. It is not possible for anyone to read more than a small part of all this literature in their lifetime.

It may seem impossible to summarize and find a common denominator in this diversity. But, as different as all these teachings are, they have one thing in common, as this slogan suggests: they all aim to reduce our attachment to the illusion of a fixed, unchanging self, and thereby free us from the suffering that this attachment causes.

As the Buddha put it in his conversation with Paharada:

> Just as the great ocean has one taste, the taste of salt, so also this Dhamma and Discipline has one taste, the taste of liberation.[17]

The liberation that the Buddha's teachings convey is the freedom from suffering and unsatisfactoriness that our ego attachment creates. The way to freedom is through self-transcendence, by identifying more and more with a 'we' instead of an 'I'. As mentioned in the introduction, this process of self-transcendence must of course always be based on a healthy sense of self-care and on positive self-esteem and dignity.

One could extend this statement and say that anything that can be called natural morality is about reducing selfishness and self-interest.[18] As biological beings, we have evolved in an 'eat or be eaten' world. This experience lives on as an attitude that we can only succeed by competing and winning over others. At the same time, there has always been a cultural and spiritual counterforce to temper and balance our natural selfish tendencies, so that we can cooperate in smaller or larger groups and in order to best serve our common interests.

The Buddha's teachings offer ways to overcome self-centredness and egoism. Whichever school or movement we practise in – Theravada, Mahayana, Vajrayana, Zen, Dzogchen, Mahamudra, or Western Buddhism – we can expect to reduce our self-centredness and egotism.

If this doesn't happen, something is wrong. Unfortunately, spiritual teachings can be hijacked and appropriated by the ego and reinforce narcissistic tendencies, rather than the opposite. If we see such a tendency in ourselves or in others, we can be sure that it is the result not of genuine Dharma practice but of an erroneous one.

Reflection

A self-test

Have I become more generous since I started practising?
Do I spontaneously think more about the welfare of others and not always first and foremost about myself?

Dhardo Rinpoche, considered by some to be a living bodhisattva, once said: 'If you don't know what to do, give something to another.' It can be anything, and it is so easy. Simply give something or do something for another or others or for the situation.

Slogan Twenty: Of the Two Witnesses, Stick to the Most Important One

It is important to listen to the judgement of others: that is the first of the two witnesses. But it is even more important to rely on your own judgement. After all, other people can't read your mind, nor do they have all the facts they would need to know what is best for you to do.

Wise people are therefore careful to advise others what to do. They are also careful to evaluate or judge the actions of others.

So the most important witness is our own judgement. This requires us to be honest with ourselves and to not turn a blind eye to our faults and shortcomings. After all, what is the point of telling yourself that you have made more progress than you actually have?

When we reflect on our own thoughts, feelings, and actions, we have everything to gain from being completely honest. If we find that we fail to live up to our own standards and that we are more driven by greed and ill will than we could wish, we have all the more to work on and can see this as an incentive to continue deepening our practice.

By contrast, to the extent that we feel that our thoughts,

feelings, and actions actually live up to our aspirations, we will feel a lightness and joy that come with having a clear conscience.

Jamgön Kongtrül writes in his commentary that we can notice progress in the lojong training when we realize that we are not ashamed of or embarrassed by our states of mind.

Milarepa emphasized the importance of personal judgement when he famously said: 'My religion is to live – and die – without regret.'[19]

Reflection

Do you feel less ashamed?

This is a very good and concrete test, because, if we think about our lives, there are certainly plenty of times when we feel a bit ashamed or blame ourselves for not living up to our ideals or something like that. If we really feel less ashamed and if we're more forgiving, that is a clear sign that the practice is bearing fruit.

So allow yourself to settle down for a while, let your mind become quiet, and sit with your body and breath for a while. Let your experience come into awareness, all the sensations in your body, the sounds around you, your thoughts and feelings. Allow them all space to just be there. Then turn your attention inwards and rest in your centre, your heart, and then ask the question: since I started practising (in the last months or years), have I felt less ashamed? Has self-blame lessened?

Notice your inner responses, the feeling you get. You don't need to analyze or comment on your experience – just note it and hold it. If you receive an affirmative answer to these questions, you can, if you wish, reflect on how this might have come about.

Slogan Twenty-One: Always Keep a Joyful Mind

This sounds wonderful, doesn't it? But is it realistic to always maintain a joyful mind? It is, of course, not something that can be done by sheer effort. Instead, it is something that arises as the result of years of training the mind and consciousness.

A clear conscience is one of the cornerstones of a joyful mind. The ability to see difficulties and hardships as opportunities for growth and development is another. Wisdom and insight, the ability to see the relativity – in the deepest sense, the emptiness – of all ideas and appearances, are a third.

If we train our minds in the right way, we should find that, over time, we become happier and lighter in spirit. What we previously experienced as adversity and difficulty no longer weighs us down or affects us in the same way.

Slogan Twenty-Two: You Are Well Trained If You Can Practise Even When Distracted

'A skilled horseman does not fall from his horse, even when he is distracted', writes Jamgön Kongtrül, commenting on this slogan.[20]

Measuring the Effects of Our Practice

All learning follows a certain pattern. First of all, we must become aware of what we do not know or understand. This is followed by a phase where we start learning something new or developing a new skill. We then pay close attention to what we are learning, and our skills depend on concentration and conscious effort. Finally, we get to the stage where we have incorporated the knowledge or skill to such an extent that we don't always think about what we know. We just do it. We don't rely on conscious effort anymore.

This also applies to training in mindfulness and compassion. Even when we are distracted by external events, we retain a basic awareness and our response to everything that happens in life is informed by the mindfulness and compassion that we have built up through previous training.

Point Six

Specific Commitments in Relation to Others

The preceding points have dealt with how we train our own mind: in meditation and between meditations, when we face difficulties, as an overall practice for our whole life, and how we notice the effects of the training.

The next part of the training, slogans twenty-three to thirty-eight, deals with how we apply wisdom and compassion in different situations that arise in relation to others.

Many of the slogans are grammatically negative and tell us what we *should not do*, rather than what we *should do*. In this way, they have the character of precepts.[21] They are meant to help us catch ourselves in different situations when we are about to do something that is not so skilful: 'Oh yes, I shouldn't do that.' At the same time, there is always a corresponding positive aspect to such precepts. When we do not automatically react according to habitual patterns, a space simultaneously opens up for more conscious, creative responses.

Slogan Twenty-Three: Stick to the Three Basic Principles at All Times

The three principles are: *sticking to your previous promises*, *not trying to stand out*, and *not training one-sidedly*. They represent some general qualities that we need to keep in mind as we practise.

Geshe Chekawa emphasizes the importance of sticking to your previous vows and commitments once you start practising lojong. As a Buddhist, you may have taken vows to practise according to certain ethical precepts. If you start to think that you are practising at a more advanced level, you may see it as less important to follow rules that you consider more conventional. 'Now I am a bodhisattva who puts others before myself, so now I don't have to worry about following these old rules.' In this context, indulgence in the use of alcohol and in sex is notorious, and several famous Dharma teachers have been guilty of it, both historically and more recently. Chekawa warns against such an attitude, which can be a form of conceit.

Another pitfall that Chekawa warns against is if we try to excel in self-sacrificing actions and selfless behaviour, in a way that can be perceived as conspicuous and boastful. If we do this, the effect of our training is the opposite of what is intended. Instead of reducing our egocentricity, we reinforce it.

The third instruction is to avoid training one-sidedly, and instead be balanced in what we do. An example given by Chekawa is where we are very generous and self-sacrificing towards family and friends, but stingy and hostile towards strangers. The reverse can also be true. There are those who make great efforts to help the vulnerable and needy somewhere far away in the world, but are uninterested or unwilling to help those closer to home.

Another form of imbalance can be if we are good at giving things up and living a very ascetic life, but at the same time we are stingy with our time and energy when it comes to volunteering and helping others in some concrete and practical way.

In all these respects we need to endeavour to practise in as balanced and comprehensive a way as possible. Some of the slogans refer to general approaches, others to typical pitfalls where it is easy to act selfishly without realizing it.

Slogan Twenty-Four: Change Your Attitude but Stay Natural

The attitude referred to here is our ingrained tendency in any situation to think of ourselves first – our own needs, our own interests. Lojong is about changing that attitude so that we start to think about the needs and interests of others first.

But the second part of the sentence is also important. We should do things for others in a way that is natural and relaxed. It is not about acting the martyr and giving up a lot of things for the sake of others, while we're grumbling inside. Our care for others should not be an expression of self-hatred. What we do for others, we should do with ease and joy because it is what we want to do and what first comes to mind.

We should also avoid all overt gestures and ostentatious behaviour when doing things for others. We should be discreet when practising lojong, preferably so that no one notices we are doing it. Others may simply note: 'That was a nice thing to do', or just seem to be happy and satisfied in their contact with us. Or they may not notice anything and just take it for granted when we do something for them. It doesn't really matter whether they show gratitude or not; what matters is whether we realize that what we are doing benefits them.

Slogan Twenty-Five: Don't Talk About Other People's Defects

Geshe Chekawa's original formulation involves not talking about lost body parts, such as whether someone is one-eyed, one-armed, or one-legged. Chekawa spent several years working with people living with leprosy, so lojong was for a long time referred to as 'leprosy training'. Leprosy leads to a loss of pain sensitivity, resulting in body parts becoming damaged and sometimes falling off. It is possible that Chekawa's experience of living with lepers influenced the formulation of this sentence.

Most of us probably take it for granted that we shouldn't speak disparagingly about other people's disabilities or defects. But, on a more subtle level, we can sometimes talk about others' stupidity or psychological difficulties in a way that does not show genuine concern for them. We may do this out of thoughtlessness, or because it makes us and those we talk to look or feel better and smarter.

In the case of other Dharma practitioners, this tendency to gossip and make derogatory judgements may relate to deficiencies in their practice, such as their inability to sit quietly and concentrate in meditation, or their disregard for ethical rules and standards, such as eating meat or drinking alcohol, if they are expected to refrain from doing so.

Specific Commitments in Relation to Others

If such shortcomings do not affect anyone else, there is no need to talk about them, unless the person themselves is interested in and open to discussing any difficulties they have in their practice.

Slogan Twenty-Six: Don't Speculate on the Intentions of Others

This slogan is similar to the previous one, but is mainly about our tendency to dwell on the faults and shortcomings of others. It is particularly common in our time with the emphasis on critical thinking.

Critical thinking is one thing; finding fault is quite another. The balanced view means keeping an open mind and refraining from judging others based on what we speculate might be true. The only things we can evaluate are the words and actions of others. We cannot read their minds, and do not know their motives for what they say and do. Even if they do things we think are wrong, there may be reasons why they act in that way. We simply don't know.

The slogan refers primarily to how we relate to our Dharma friends and the shortcomings in their practice that we perceive. According to Geshe Chekawa, we should first examine ourselves and see if the shortcomings we notice might actually reflect shortcomings in ourselves. This is good psychology. What we resent in others is often what we don't want to recognize in ourselves.

If we come to the conclusion that others are doing wrong, we should be compassionate and caring about them, rather than distant and judgemental. We can try to help them if they are receptive, or at least hope that they will come to terms with whatever is behind their inappropriate behaviour.

We should strive for an open and nuanced view of the faults and shortcomings of others, which also means being wary of uncritical admiration and blind trust in others. This is particularly important in spiritual contexts, not least in Tibetan Buddhism, where there is a strong focus on teachers as indispensable to effective practice. Just as constant fault-finding can be an obstacle, so can credulity and blindness to the faults of others.

Reflection

Relationship with spiritual teachers

It can be useful to explore your views and attitudes towards your spiritual teachers and role models. These don't have to be people you have direct contact with; it could even be someone who is not alive, although the reflection is most potent when it is done with someone who is alive. How do you view the Dalai Lama, for example? Most people have not met him and shaken hands. But everyone seems to have an image and perception of him. Examine whether the image you have is realistic or somewhat romanticized. Can you imagine him making mistakes sometimes?

Of course, it is natural to look up to and admire and even revere people who we feel are much further along the path than we are. It's a helpful quality and even essential if we are to connect with and develop the more elevated aspects of our potential. It is only when we are able to see certain qualities embodied in another, at least to some degree, that those qualities are truly awakened in ourselves. It may be someone's greater awareness or compassion or thoughtfulness or something else.

It is important to allow ourselves to feel and be moved by this deeper trust, but we should remember that they are also human.

Slogan Twenty-Seven: Work on the Main Poisons First

The poisons referred to are the *kleshas* – the mental 'poisons' which, according to Buddhism, are the causes of suffering. The basic poisons are *greed*, *ill will*, and *unawareness*.[22] The unawareness referred to here is a deeply rooted unwillingness to see reality as it is, for example that our actions have consequences for others. In addition to these three, *pride* and *envy* are sometimes included in the *kleshas*.

They can be seen as poisons because they have an unhealthy influence on our lives. They create stress, worry, anxiety, and depression that can actually make us ill in the long run. They also poison our relationships.

The intention of this slogan is that we should first work on our main weaknesses. If greed is our main weakness and we tend to hurt ourselves or others under the influence of greed, that is what we should work on, even though we may be quite good-natured and kind in other respects. If, however, we are well disciplined and find it easy to give things up but are easily irritated and moody, our first job is to work on ill will.

We may have a tendency to do the opposite by reinforcing the good qualities we already have, while ignoring our main weaknesses. The negative states of mind that correspond to the *kleshas* are interrelated so that, if one type is weakened, the others are also weakened. It is the same with positive states of mind. Love and kindness reinforce feelings like generosity and gratitude, and vice versa.

Slogan Twenty-Eight: Drop All Expectations of Results

An overall purpose of practice is to free us from all hopes and fears. Hope and fear are about looking into the future, mentally travelling through time, and imagining different possible outcomes.

Such mental time travel may have a limited value and give us direction, but in general we should try to be present here and now in our practice.

If we fantasize and dwell on all the wonderful possible fruits we could enjoy on the path, such as happiness and inner peace, or even insight and awakening, it will have an inhibiting effect on our practice.

It is better to let go of all such thoughts, and instead enjoy the moments of stillness and contentment that inevitably arise from time to time. Instead of seeing awakening or enlightenment as a distant goal, which we make a lot of sacrifices to achieve, we can see our spontaneous moments of compassion and equanimity as small moments of awakening.

As time passes, the moments of awakening will become more and more numerous. One of the main teachings of Zen master Dogen[23] was that practice and awakening are one and the same thing. To meditate is to be awakened, to be awakened is to meditate. We can understand this as awakening being a natural state of awareness, which is the same state that we practise in our meditation.

Slogan Twenty-Nine: Avoid Toxic Foods

The food referred to here is not ordinary food, but spiritual nourishment. This can be meditation, knowledge transmitted through books, or guidance from teachers. Like physical food, such nourishment can build up our mental strength and emotional resources.

But the food can also be poisoned if the knowledge and skills foster and reinforce self-preoccupation – the opposite effect of what we intend in practising the Dharma.

Unfortunately, it is a common phenomenon that spiritual practice fuels narcissism. The admiration and worship that teachers can be subject to can be a strong temptation. People who may have initially been seekers because of fragile self-esteem are suddenly given an opportunity to shine and excel as role models for others. What originally served as healthy nourishment becomes a drug that poisons the person's life, just as it ultimately poisons the lives of the followers who flock around such a teacher.

Slogan Thirty: Don't Be So Predictable

We all have a tendency to react to events in life through familiar and habitual patterns. Much of the time we are on 'autopilot', and what we do is largely predictable. This slogan is about being creative rather than reactive in our approach to the world.[24]

Sometimes it is as if we wake up and realize that things can be done differently. Or we meet another person who says or does something unexpected. Like when your debit card at the supermarket checkout isn't working and you're standing there with all the goods on the conveyor belt and can't pay, and the customer behind you says: 'It's okay, I'll pay for your groceries.'

It can be simple things like actually talking about how we really feel when a colleague asks this at morning coffee break, instead of saying: 'Yes, it's all fine', when it's not.

These moments when we are not so predictable are moments when we are authentic and present. You could also say that they are moments when we are fully alive. Any time we act in a completely predictable way, it is as if we were already dead.

Another meaning of this phrase is that we should avoid the tendency to always keep track of pluses and minuses in our relationships. We expect to receive as much as we give, of money and of our time and energy. If we don't, we tend to become dissatisfied and may distance ourselves from that person. But the slogan asks us to give people a second chance, not to see people as unchangeable.

Specific Commitments in Relation to Others

Slogan Thirty-One: Don't Speak Ill of Others

Speaking ill of others means talking about others in a way that damages their reputation or standing in the eyes of others. It is something we do to strengthen our own position in relation to the person we are slandering. It is a kind of power game that we should not engage in.

This does not mean that we can never criticize another person's views or actions. Sometimes we may need to do so, to counteract what we perceive as a negative influence, or simply to clarify our own position on the issue.

But, when we feel compelled to criticize another person, we should examine our motives. Is our intention really constructive, or are we really just engaging in gossip or malicious slander?

These days it is so easy to ruin a person's reputation and damage their social relationships on social media. We may not realize how much suffering we can cause in this way. A particularly insidious form of speaking ill of others is when we use sarcasm and mockery under the guise of humour.

Slogan Thirty-Two: Don't Ambush Others

Many of the slogans have the same structure: a striking image with a concrete meaning that we can imagine was used by farmers and nomads in twelfth-century Tibet. At the same time, they are metaphors for mental attitudes that we can adopt just as much here and in our time.

We may not literally ambush our enemies with guns blazing, but we can wait for opportunities to attack a competitor or rival in more subtle ways. When the person shows a weakness, or when we are suddenly backed by others, we can be tempted to take the opportunity to pounce on the person to gain an advantage over them.

A common reason why we lie in ambush and wait for an opportunity to attack a person is because we want to get back at them for old grievances. It is nothing more than a desire for revenge. We can ask ourselves why we want revenge and what we have to gain from it. The likelihood is that revenge on our part will lead to further retaliation from the victim and an escalating conflict. If we have really been wronged, it is better to seek some form of reconciliation that is acceptable to both parties.

Slogan Thirty-Three: Don't Push Things to the Point of Pain

If we do choose to criticize the opinions or actions of others, and on good grounds, it is important that we do so constructively. We should always distinguish between a fact and a person. This means that we can criticize an opinion, behaviour, or action, but without deliberately offending or degrading the person concerned. It is an approach that follows naturally from the realization that there is no single and unchanging self behind opinions or actions.

However, even if we perceive it that way and our criticism is about opinions and actions and not about an 'evil' or 'bad' person, the other person may not see it that way. They may still be offended and upset, and experience the criticism as an attack on their person.

If this happens, we should back off and not push the issue to its 'pain point'. We have done what we intended; we have made our point. If the person can't take the feedback in a way that is helpful to them, it is better that we drop the issue, explain that we didn't intend to hurt them but just wanted to express our views on something they said or did.

The slogan also tells us to be careful about criticizing people for things they are particularly sensitive about. This is especially relevant in close relationships where people know each other well, including weaknesses.

It is also one of the reasons why it is good to recognize our own weaknesses. We are then less likely to be caught off-guard and retaliate if we are criticized or challenged. When we know our weaknesses, we are not as easily hurt and can more easily see whether the criticism is true and relevant or not.

Slogan Thirty-Four: Don't Put the Burden of a Dzo on an Ox

A dzo is a cross between an ox and a yak. When the Dalai Lama fled Tibet from the Chinese occupation in 1959, he came riding across the Indian border on a dzo.

A dzo is a particularly powerful pack animal. An ox is also strong, but nowhere near as strong as a dzo. Placing the burden intended for a dzo on an ox is therefore not fair to the ox.

Similarly, we ourselves should not place burdens on others that we are better suited to bear ourselves. This slogan is about not shirking responsibility by letting others carry more than they can handle. It can also refer to our tendency to dump our own suffering on others. We all have a tendency to want to talk things through when we are struggling. Of course, being open even about what is difficult is good if it allows others to sympathize and support us. But we must be careful not to drag others down and drain them by talking too much about our suffering. It is primarily our own burden to bear. If we have practised lojong for a while, we also have the strength to cope with a heavier burden. We have to be especially careful not to lay our burden on someone else when we know they may not be able to manage it.

Slogan Thirty-Five: Don't Strive to Be First to the Top

There are different interpretations and translations of this slogan, but the idea is that we should not strive to stand out. Almost all of us have a need to prove that we are smart, fast, and capable – we really want to be the first to reach the top.

There is nothing inherently wrong with being smart and fast, or with striving to use our abilities as best we can. But what lies behind our desire to always be the smartest and fastest? And how do we react when we are not?

A good way to approach achievements is to concentrate on the performance, not the outcome. It is a good strategy because we concentrate on what we can actually influence. We can influence what we do, not how others perform or how others perceive our performance.

It is also a way to counteract our self-centredness. It does not matter whether we win or lose, whether we are better or worse than others. What matters is the performance itself, the feeling of doing something good based on our conditions.

'Give all the victory to others, take all the loss on yourself' was the phrase that brought Geshe Chekawa to the teaching that gave rise to lojong. Just as when Jesus says that, if someone strikes us, we should turn the other cheek, it is not to be taken too literally. It's a call to stop and examine our habitual reaction patterns. Why is it so important to win and avoid losses? What does it mean to win or to lose?

Slogan Thirty-Six: Don't Act with an Ulterior Motive

We are masterful at gaining advantage through flattery and posturing, through pretended kindness and caring. In such social games, how skilled we are at the game and whether or not people see through us are crucial. What stops us from playing these social games is insight, when we see through the basic assumption that gaining advantages at the expense of others is something desirable.

We often have mixed motives for the things we do. This is also true when we practise the Dharma and lojong. There may be a genuine desire for liberation from suffering for oneself and others, alongside other less wholesome motives such as a desire to be appreciated and admired. Up to a point, this need not be wrong. We may initially need to strengthen low self-esteem only to eventually be in a position to transcend it. But we should pay attention to whether there are such elements in our motivation to practise.

Slogan Thirty-Seven: Don't Turn Gods into Demons

This slogan continues with variations on the same theme. We must be careful not to turn our high ideals into means of self-glorification. Gods are characterized by qualities such as superhuman strength, wisdom, or goodness, qualities that we aspire to. The gods of our time are mostly fictional characters, ranging from the superheroes in movies to more complex and subtle characters in fiction. Our idols and heroes in sport, music, and popular culture can sometimes also take on a godlike status.

Hero worship seems to correspond to a deep human need. In the spiritual sphere, idolatry is directed towards various gurus and masters. There is, of course, nothing wrong with seeking out role models and guides; on the contrary, it is necessary for an authentic and living understanding of spiritual teachings. But there are obvious dangers as well. We should beware of the tendency to idealize teachers. As a rule, there is a shadow side to their personality, which it is good for us to discover, sooner rather than later. We should also perhaps stop looking for the perfect teacher, and instead settle for a teacher who clearly knows more than us and can help us along the way.

We run an even greater risk if we find ourselves in a situation where we are subject to the idolatry of others. Being the bearer of the 'guru archetype' without being intoxicated and seduced by the projection requires a high degree of integrity and maturity. We should only take on such a role if we genuinely feel prepared to do so out of real compassion and concern for others. If we deceive ourselves and it becomes an ego project instead, there is a big risk that it will end badly for everyone involved.

Slogan Thirty-Eight: Don't Exploit the Misfortune of Others for Your Own Benefit

This is also a way in which our cunning and crafty minds can work. One example given by Geshe Chekawa is when we await an inheritance from a relative and secretly rejoice in the relative's poor health and supposed imminent demise. Another example he gives is when the death of a prominent teacher can open the way for our own advancement in the spiritual hierarchy.

These may seem to be rather crude examples, but, if we are honest, most of us can recognize situations where we have thought that someone else's misfortune could be to our own advantage, even if it is just a fleeting thought that we quickly dismiss.

The point is that even such a fleeting thought is an indication that we are still sometimes self-centred, that 'selfing' still has us in its grip. In such a situation, we should kindly acknowledge what we are doing, and use some antidote to self-centredness, reflect on the situation of the one affected by misfortune or suffering, and see what we can do to help them.

Exercise

 Rejoicing in merits

There are many ways to counteract self-centredness, and perhaps the easiest is to simply be generous with your time and skills because there is almost always something you can give or share. For example, when you arrive at someone's home or in a communal setting, make it a habit to ask if there is anything you can do to help.

There is a practice in Buddhism that not only reduces our self-absorption but also makes us appreciate others more, their good qualities and all the good they do. The practice is called 'rejoicing in merit'. You can do it with colleagues or friends, or in other social groupings. And you can choose to focus on one person in the group so that everyone rejoices in that person's merits, or you can rejoice in everyone in the group, perhaps saying a few things about each person. You can also do this exercise on your own, but it is best to do it with others so that you can actually express your appreciation. You could also write an appreciative message or letter to someone. Here's how to do it:

First, take a moment to just think about the person: think about what you appreciate about them, their good qualities, and the good they do in the world. You don't have to turn a blind eye to their weaknesses – because we all have weaknesses – but, for now, focus on their 'merits' and positive aspects. Now, when I think of a particular friend of mine, I think of his good mood, his positive

Specific Commitments in Relation to Others

attitude towards life, even though it is far from easy, that he is almost always laughing, that he can easily laugh at his own mistakes and shortcomings (with warmth in his voice), that he often gets in touch and wants to talk, that he can easily empathize, and, because he knows me so well and is well aware of both my weaknesses and strengths, he doesn't hesitate to pull my leg when that's needed, but also to remind me of all the good things I do and my strengths. These are some of the things that spontaneously came to mind when thinking about my friend.

You can write down the characteristics you think of, perhaps with examples. Notice how this exercise makes you feel. From time to time in your daily life, you can come back to this and remember the good qualities of others. You may want to suggest to your friends that you do this exercise together.

Point Seven
Guidelines for Lojong

Point seven describes further aspects of the training in bodhicitta and practical compassion. As with the previous slogans, we can read and reflect on one or a few slogans each day, and then try to apply the message to daily life. Many of the slogans overlap, and it can sometimes be difficult to see how an individual slogan fits into the overall structure. It isn't even certain that the creators of lojong cared much about the overall structure. Perhaps they saw it more as a loose framework that they could fill with insightful lessons. Some of the things they wanted to emphasize could well be repeated from slightly different angles.

In the final part of lojong, we encounter twenty-one slogans that provide tips on a few things we should consider in our daily practice. One of the advantages of lojong is that we can practise even if we live a very active life. We can also benefit from practising lojong in times of difficulty, such as illness or other crises.

Slogan Thirty-Nine: Do Everything with the Same Purpose

The idea here is to try to hold on to a conscious intention in everything we do. We may have a clear intention to develop mindfulness and compassion when we meditate or do other exercises that we see as our practice.

But most of the day is spent on activities for which we do not have the same clear intention. We work, socialize, eat, read, or watch TV, but we usually don't think much about the purpose of what we are doing.

The point of lojong is that all these activities can become part of our practice if they are imbued with an overall purpose. Everything we do can become an expression of bodhicitta, the will to awaken for the sake of all beings. Another way to put it is that the purpose of everything we do is to reduce suffering and promote happiness in the world. We do this by working to ensure that those who are hungry are fed, that those who are sick are helped so they can be cured or cared for, that those who are struggling at least meet someone who listens to and understands them. We can't help everyone, but we can help a few.

We also need to help ourselves and meet our own needs. These needs can include sometimes being alone and having time for reflection and meditation, but also relaxing and doing something undemanding such as listening to music or watching a film on TV.

Bodhicitta involves not only a desire to reduce suffering, but also a desire to reduce *the cause* of suffering. Since the cause of suffering is ultimately our self-centredness, the overall purpose also includes striving to reduce both our own self-centredness and that of others.

It is a difficult task that requires wisdom and experience. The most important way to do this is to lead by example. By being selfless and supportive, we can inspire others to do the same. By demonstrating patience and calm confidence in the face of trials, we can show that there is no need to be governed by hope or despair when things don't go as planned. By showing that we are willing to share difficulties and hardships with others, we reduce our own self-centredness while helping others to gain perspective on their suffering.

Slogan Forty: Meet All Opposition with the Same Intention

Geshe Chekawa's original text mentions feeling a resistance when we are criticized or slandered, and as a result beginning to doubt our own capabilities. We begin to question whether we are really making any progress in our practice, and perhaps even to question the whole point of training in mindfulness, wisdom, and compassion.

What we should do then is to shift the focus from ourselves to others. We can think of those who through unskilful actions create misfortune for themselves and others. We apply the principle of taking in suffering and giving out relief in order to help others, for example by doing tonglen meditation.

What we then do is shift the focus from *my* practice to *our* practice. We are not practising on our own, but together with everyone else. We are not islands: we are closely linked to each other. And we all basically want the same thing – to be happy and free from suffering.

Exchanging oneself for others is one of the underlying principles of the lojong teachings as a whole. Once again, this doesn't mean forgetting ourselves; rather, we correct an imbalance of seeing our own needs as much more important than those of others, in favour of seeing our own and others' needs as equally important.

Slogan Forty-One: Two Activities: One at the Beginning and One at the End

Two times of the day are particularly suitable for practice: when we wake up in the morning and before we go to sleep at night. If we do not have much time, we can at least think two thoughts. In the morning when we get out of bed, we can think: 'Today I will do things that are of benefit and that bring happiness to myself and others.' When we go to bed, we can think: 'Everything I have done of value today, to the best of my ability, I dedicate to the welfare of all living beings.'

If we have a little more time, we can spend some time in the morning reflecting on the training in compassion. For example, we can choose to reflect on one or a few of the lojong slogans. If we can, it is excellent to set aside half an hour or more for meditation in the morning. We can engage in the meditation practices we have learned such as mindfulness of breathing, loving-kindness meditation, tonglen – giving and receiving – or some other form of meditation that includes visualization or mantra recitation.

A *sadhana* is a personal meditation practice that expresses an overall intention or purpose in our life. If this overall intention is to develop bodhicitta, the will to awaken for all, we can design our daily meditation practice to reinforce this intention. In all daily activities, we can try to remind ourselves of the intention. Here the slogans can be helpful. Eventually everything we do will be imbued with bodhicitta, and there will no longer be a difference between ordinary life and practice.

In the evening, before we fall asleep, we can look back on the day and reflect on when we were able to keep our intention and when we might have temporarily lost it. Why is it that we sometimes lose touch with our intention? Do strong emotions sometimes take over and, if so, which emotions? Or do we get so lost in our thoughts or activities that we forget the purpose of what we are doing?

Take a moment to think about these questions. What are the patterns in your life?

Slogan Forty-Two: Whichever of the Two Occurs, Remain Patient

The two referred to here are success and misfortune. We tend to experience life as a sequence of events where what we perceive as successes alternate with what we perceive as setbacks.

Sometimes the successes come one after the other, and we may be tempted to believe that this is how it will always be. We get an interesting and well-paid job, we live in a loving relationship, we are healthy, and our loved ones are also well.

However, the truth is that good fortune can change at any time. In fact, this is inevitable. Sooner or later, success turns into adversity, profit turns into loss. You can't always just win! Unemployment, financial problems, and illness can strike anyone at any time. Often, both success and failure are due to factors beyond our control.

The slogan urges us to be patient whether we face success or misfortune. Patience in the face of success may sound a bit strange. But the idea is not to get caught up in the wave of success and later suffer from hubris – according to ancient mythology, what happened when a person wanted to emulate or surpass the gods. Anyone caught up in *hubris* would sooner or later suffer the punishment of the gods, *nemesis*.

Buddhism talks about the eight worldly winds: pleasure and pain, gain and loss, praise and blame, fame and infamy. We should try to hold on to our general direction in life, whether we are fortunate enough to sail with the wind or have to cruise against it.

Slogan Forty-Three: Watch These Two, Even at the Risk of Your Life

This slogan refers to the two vows that can be taken in Mahayana Buddhism: going for refuge and the bodhisattva vow.

Going for refuge, which is common to all Buddhists, involves committing oneself to the Buddha, Dharma, and Sangha. These refuges are sometimes referred to as 'the three jewels'. The Buddha represents the enlightened ideal to which one aspires, the Dharma represents his teachings, and the Sangha represents those who embody the ideal in varying degrees, as wells as the community of all those who follow the same ideal.

Guidelines for Lojong

So what does it mean to take refuge in the three jewels? You could say that you turn to the Buddha, his teachings, and the community, again and again, seeking inspiration, support, and guidance. Going for or seeking refuge is an emotional commitment – what you turn to, what you put your heart on and invest your energy in.

In a sense, we go for refuge to many things in our lives, but often to things that will not return or match our investment. However, the three jewels are said to be 'true refuges' because we can rely on them and because they are enduring ideals and values in a world that is otherwise unstable and uncertain.

The bodhisattva vow is a promise to strive for awakening for the sake of all beings and to achieve the goals represented by the practice of lojong.

Generally speaking, these two vows correspond to two commitments: to work on one's own personal development and to work for the good of all living beings. The vows can be formalized and taken in a ceremonial way at the time of ordination. But it is above all a personal commitment that we make in our hearts.

The wording of the slogan is strong, and most of us will not face situations where we risk our lives because of our promises. But historically and globally, this is not uncommon. We can imagine circumstances where others force us to act in a way that goes against our beliefs, such as killing innocent people in war. How would we act in such a case? It is of course very difficult to know until we are in such a situation, but we can try to imagine what it would be like. The slogans urge us to stick to our promises in circumstances like these, even if it means risking our own lives.

Reflection

What do you take refuge in?

We 'take refuge' in a variety of things in our lives, and expect them to bring us fulfilment, happiness, and security. But do they really?

Take a moment to think about what you rely on in life, where you put your longing and hope. What do you take refuge in in your life? What things do you expect to bring you security and happiness in life?

Is it pleasure, success, esteem, truth, science, art? Or perhaps relationships, work, or family? Or material things like your home, car, boat, gadgets, your country house, or something else? Reflect on these questions for a while, and be as honest as you can. See what comes to mind.

What things and people do you feel you can really trust? Think about what gives you deep satisfaction and what makes you feel safe. Feel free to write down your reflections.

Slogan Forty-Four: Practise the Three Difficulties

The three difficulties refer to the three characteristics of negative mental states that make them difficult to overcome.

Firstly, they appear suddenly. Without knowing how it happened, we are suddenly filled with anger, envy, or greed. Our first task is therefore to be mindful of and alert to the first signs of such states of mind. We are then in a position to prevent them from finding a foothold and developing.

The second difficulty with negative states of mind is that, once they have gained a hold on us, they are hard to get rid of. They often act as mental poisons that we find difficult to get out of our system. What we can do is examine the state of mind and identify what it is really about. If we are angry, we can try to see if there really is a basis for the anger. Have we interpreted the situation correctly? For example, if we are upset about what someone has said to us, are we sure what their intention was? Is it something really worth getting upset about, or are we overreacting because our ego is a bit bruised?

Finally, negative mental states are difficult to manage because they tend to occur over and over again. We therefore need to get to the bottom of them and examine their origins. We can do this by attacking the very root of the poison, by seeing how their cause lies in our basic self-centredness and ignorance. The most effective approach, but also the most difficult, is to apply an understanding of absolute bodhicitta. We can free ourselves from all forms of negative states by seeing how thoughts and feelings are empty of intrinsic nature – that they are like dreams or illusions that arise from temporary conditions and disappear as easily as they arise.

Slogan Forty-Five: Create the Three Main Conditions

The first of these three main conditions for effective practice is having a personal teacher. This is something that is very much emphasized in Tibetan Buddhism, just as the importance of spiritual friendship is emphasized in other Buddhist traditions. While the study of books and personal meditation are good and necessary, they are not enough. A teacher can pass on their own experience and adapt their teaching to our needs. Above all, a teacher can recognize when we are going astray and deceiving ourselves, and help us to see the blind spots in our psyche. Spiritual friends can do the same even if they do not formally have the role of a teacher. It is not always easy to find experienced and reliable teachers. What we can do at first is to seek out a community and find friends who can mirror and help us.

The second condition for effective practice is that we are motivated to practise. Without motivation, it is difficult to do anything at all. To get up and meditate every morning, day in and day out, year after year, requires strong motivation. Motivation varies naturally over time, and it is an art to practise in such a way that we preserve and maintain it.

Finally, we also need some practical conditions. Even if we have a teacher and are highly motivated to practise, it can be difficult if we do not have the material conditions. We need financial conditions in the form of a roof over our heads and food for the day. We need to live in a social context where our practice is accepted, such as having the opportunity to meditate relatively undisturbed for a while during the day. We also need time. If all our waking time is taken up by work and other obligations, it is difficult to practise, especially to meditate. In this respect also, it can be an advantage to belong to a practising community of some kind, a sangha, in order to get help in creating good conditions.

If we have these three prerequisites for effective practice, we can remind ourselves that it is not a given, and thereby strengthen our motivation to make good use of our favourable conditions. If we do not have access to all three, we can try to establish the missing condition. We can actively try to find a teacher, or spiritual friends, who we really believe can help us. Or we can make changes in our lives, to free up time or other resources if that is what we lack. If motivation is lacking, we can try to work on strengthening it.

Geshe Chekawa also emphasizes that we should think compassionately about all those who are not as well placed to practise as we might be. Poverty and other social circumstances can make it very difficult to practise at all. In a traditional society, meditation is almost entirely reserved for monks and nuns, or others who have chosen to live as hermits. In our modern society, the situation is different and the limitations we have are largely due to our life choices, such as whether we have chosen to have children, establish a professional career, or buy a house. However, we can all be struck by illness, financial difficulties, or other forms of adversity that limit our ability to practise.

Slogan Forty-Six: Make Sure the Three Never Subside

The three that we must guard against diminishing are commitment and devotion to our teachers, enthusiasm for learning and practice, and the discipline to practise what we have learned.

Devotion to our teachers is not about blind trust or idolatry, but about being grateful for what we have learned from others. Even if we have acquired much of our knowledge through reading, it is people who have put in the time and effort to write the books and share their knowledge and experience. Reminding ourselves of how much we owe others is a way to counteract complacency and arrogance. This applies not only to spiritual teachers but also to all those from whom we have learned, and especially those who have mentored us in the difficult art of living a good and rich life.

Enthusiasm for practising what we have learned naturally varies over time. It is therefore important that we pay attention to when this enthusiasm fades. We can then try to find our way back to the original sources of our inspiration. It could be texts we have read in the past that we know inspire us. It could be friends who remind us of what makes us tick. Sometimes we can regain our motivation by supporting a friend who is going through a difficult time. Other sources of inspiration can be nature, art, or literature that reconnects us with what is important and significant in life.

When enthusiasm fails, discipline is all the more important. If we decide to meditate every day, we should continue with it even if we don't always feel like meditating and sometimes doubt its value. Discipline is about creating good habits, and in order to build good habits we sometimes have to overcome resistance. It can help to focus our efforts as much as possible on what is most important. Dilgo Khyentse Rinpoche points out that bodhicitta is the most important of the 84,000 teachings traditionally attributed to the Buddha. So all we really need to do is practise bodhicitta by recalling one of the lojong slogans every day.

Slogan Forty-Seven: Keep the Three Inseparable

Body, speech, and mind are the three that we should keep integrated and aligned. This is the traditional division of our psychophysical organism in Buddhism. When we train in compassion, it is important that we do so as embodied beings, that it is not just thought that is involved, but that speech as the expression of thought and the body as the seat of our emotions are fully involved as well.

When we meditate, we do so not only with the mind but also with the body. The posture we adopt – whether sitting cross-legged or on a chair with our back straight and hands in our lap – is an integral part of practice.

To develop the more embodied side of meditation, physical exercises such as yoga or qigong are good complements. To involve speech, we can recite mantras or inspirational verses.

It is not only in the context of exercises that might be perceived as 'spiritual' that we should keep body, speech, and mind inseparable. Ideally, we should do so in all our daily activities. Everything we think, do, and say can express harmony, joy, attention, and sensitivity.

This is also the meaning of authenticity. When body, speech, and mind are in harmony, we feel whole, and others perceive us as genuine and authentic.

Exercise

 Walking meditation

In one of the most important texts where the Buddha teaches awareness, the *Satipatthana Sutta*, he describes how you train to be aware in all activities. One is encouraged to be mindful when standing, walking, sitting, or lying down; when going to the toilet, when eating, and so on. A natural complement to sitting meditation is therefore walking meditation. Some may even find it easier or more suitable than sitting meditation. The appeal of walking meditation is that you are moving, and many people find it easier to be aware when they have a tangible physical experience. Read this simple description first, and then try it out for yourself.

First, decide where you want to do walking meditation. Outdoors is probably best, but it can also be done indoors if you have the space. Choose a place where you can walk back and forth about ten or twenty metres, on level ground and relatively undisturbed. Then start by standing still for a while. Just stand there and take in what is around you, the contact with the earth under your feet, the air you breathe and feel against your skin. Let the sounds just be there as a background. Then start walking, a little slower than usual, and feel the contact with the ground through your legs and feet. Feel how your whole body moves, how your arms swing. Let your eyes rest a bit in front of you, perhaps on the ground. You can be aware of your surroundings without looking around, but, if your eyes wander, just notice that. Similarly, if you get lost in thought or an emotion, just notice that too. As you do in sitting meditation, just come back to your body and breathing calmly.

Just walk back and forth like this, stopping for a moment each time before turning round. Take in your environment, feel that you are part of it. Be aware of being here and now, and relax. Let the walking be as natural and relaxed as possible. Let your legs, arms, and whole body relax. Do this for about ten minutes or a little longer if you wish. Before moving on to what comes next, notice how it feels in your body and mind.

I have described one way to do walking meditation, but there are of course many different ways to do it. For example, you can walk very slowly, especially when you are on a retreat. You can also decide to be aware during a certain stretch you usually walk – to the bus, to the subway, with the dog. Then decide to simply walk a little slower than usual, and enjoy being mindful in the way I described above. Sometimes you can also allow yourself the luxury of standing still, looking around, and simply being where you are, without having to accomplish or achieve anything.

Slogan Forty-Eight: Train without One-Sidedness in All Respects. It Is Crucial to Do It Comprehensively and Wholeheartedly

This slogan is about just that: not seeing the practice as something separate from the rest of our lives. In lojong one talks about meditation and post-meditation. As soon as our formal practice, such as sitting meditation, is over, post-meditation begins, where we interact with other people and the world at large. There is no activity that we cannot perform with awareness and compassion. And no situation in which we cannot practise lojong.

Slogan Forty-Nine: Always Meditate on What Causes Bitterness

This slogan appears in different variants and can be interpreted in slightly different ways. One possible interpretation is that we should not avoid situations where we are challenged or criticized. By now, we should have learned that lojong is not about avoiding difficulties. Instead of avoiding what is unpleasant and difficult, we are encouraged to face difficulties head-on and see them as opportunities for growth.

We should also pay particular attention to whether feelings of bitterness, envy, or discontent creep up on us. Such feelings can affect us deeply without us realizing it. When we become aware of such feelings, we can meditate on them and try to analyze the cause. More often than not, we may discover that the cause is basically confusion and self-centredness.

We can also reflect on what unhealthy emotions like bitterness actually are. When we discover a state of mind that we identify as bitterness, how does it feel? Where in the body is the feeling to be found? What thoughts accompany the feeling? If we let the thoughts slowly fade away, does the feeling remain? And, if so, what does it consist of?

What happens, if we are able to analyze an emotion in this way, is that what we thought was a strong and unshakeable emotion that has us in a firm grip actually dissolves. It 'self-liberates', as they say in Tibetan Buddhism. It is only to the extent that we lack clear awareness that unwanted emotions retain their grip on us.

Slogan Fifty: Don't Be Influenced by External Circumstances

When we practise lojong, we don't have to worry so much about external circumstances. From a more conventional point of view, it is only natural to try and create favourable conditions, for example for meditation. We'd like it to be peaceful and quiet around us. It is also an advantage if our basic needs are met, such as food and shelter. Ideally, we also need plenty of time.

This is one of the reasons why we go on a meditation retreat. A retreat is designed to create the best possible conditions for meditation. We may go to a retreat centre situated in a beautiful landscape, follow a programme of regular meditations and other exercises, be served healthy vegetarian or vegan food, have deep, meaningful conversations with others, and perhaps enjoy periods of silence.

Anyone who has been on a retreat knows how radically it can change your experience of meditation and Dharma practice. But there is a danger that we become too preoccupied with creating the optimal external conditions. The food may not suit us, so we are bothered by bloating and gas. The bed is too hard, and we don't feel refreshed after a night's sleep. Others in the meditation hall might move around too much for our liking, or someone catches a cold and coughs.

The advantage of lojong is that we can forget all that. We can practise compassion even if the circumstances are not the best. The message of lojong is that it can even be better if the circumstances are unfavourable.

Not being dependent on external circumstances is therefore a great freedom. Nothing can stop us from practising. Not even if we get sick, become poor, or end up in prison. We can always work with our mind and awareness, and develop compassion for others.

Slogan Fifty-One: At This Crucial Time, Practise the Essentials

The traditional Buddhist view is that we have lived an infinite number of lives before this one. In the vast majority of them, we probably didn't have the opportunity to practise the Dharma. *This crucial time* is now, in this life. We have met the Dharma, and we can practise it. Just the fact that we are learning about lojong and training in compassion presents us with a unique opportunity that most living beings that have so far existed have not had.

But we can also see that we are at a crucial time for humanity and for our planet. We have unique access to the accumulated knowledge and experience of humanity and to liberating teachings such as lojong. At the same time, many of us have the material conditions necessary for an effective practice. But we don't know how long it will last. There are many threats to our welfare, to our freedom as individuals, and to our collective survival. We have a window of opportunity right now, but we do not know for how long.

Now that we have the opportunity, we would be foolish not to practise what is most essential. Firstly, our practice is more essential than theoretical knowledge and learning. It is good to read books, but better still to meditate on the content and meaning of the teachings.

Of all good and valuable knowledge, the most important is bodhicitta. Of all the Buddha's teachings, the teaching on compassion is the most important. So this time, when we have the opportunity, let us practise bodhicitta.

Slogan Fifty-Two: Beware of Misplaced Emotions

This slogan warns against feelings or attitudes that may appear to be positive but that are in fact focused on the wrong things. Geshe Chekawa gives six such examples.

Perseverance is positive if it is aimed at developing compassion or other good qualities. But, no matter how heroically we endure adversity and hardship, it is of little value if the goal is simply power or money for personal enjoyment.

Desire is also something that can be positive if you long for peace of mind and happiness, and it acts as a driving force for change. But if it is directed towards external things, such as short-term pleasure, material possessions, or social status, it is misguided. It is misdirected in the sense that, even if we achieve what we desire, whatever it is, it does not provide the satisfaction we think it should.

Similarly, *enthusiasm* can be misplaced if we are only enthusiastic about our own successes and gains.

Chekawa also mentions that *compassion* can be misplaced when we feel sorry for a hermit who lives as an ascetic, meditating in demanding circumstances. Instead, we should have compassion for those who commit evil acts, and thus create suffering for themselves and others.

Helpfulness can also be seen as a good quality. It feels good to help others, but helping others to achieve success and gain benefits in ways that may be ethically questionable does more harm than good.

To *rejoice* in the success of others may also seem like a good thing. But, if we rejoice in superficial successes such as power and money, we may only reinforce their attachment to such things. Instead, we can try to express our goodwill by focusing on other things, on their human qualities and their potential to develop as human beings.

All these examples can be seen as *near enemies* of truly positive emotions. A few examples of *far enemies* are: despondency, disinterest, dejection, indifference, helplessness, and envy. Near enemies are more subtle and harder to detect. But, as we can see from the examples above, they can be quite destructive. They also have a tendency to turn into one of the far enemies when things don't go our way, and our true intentions are revealed.

Slogan Fifty-Three: Do Not Waver

The biggest challenge in any form of practice is to persevere even during periods when we feel resistance to practice and want to give up. If you decide to meditate every morning, sooner or later – probably sooner rather than later – you will wake up feeling that you'd like to stay in bed a little longer, or that you have so many other things to think about that you don't have time. And, when you miss one day, it easily becomes two and then the good habit is broken. Before you know it, you have forgotten your original intention and you find yourself back at square one in your training.

The nineteenth-century German philosopher Arthur Schopenhauer made an interesting observation about the nature of 'the will' when he pointed out that we can choose what we do, but we cannot choose what we want.[25]

What we can do is influence our will indirectly, as it is closely linked to and expressed in thoughts and emotions. We do this by formulating intentions based on a strong desire or expression of will that we experience in the moment. If we decide to get up the next morning to meditate, we can do it, even if the desire the next morning is just a memory from yesterday. To strengthen motivation and overcome resistance, we can recall the intention we formulated the day before, the arguments we used for ourselves, and all the previous times we thought the same thing. This is how we build habits.

To practise lojong is a big commitment that we should not take on lightly. Once we decide, we need to have a very generous horizon for the commitment. Of course, we should evaluate our practice from time to time and ask ourselves whether we are making progress, whether we feel more compassionate, freer, and happier as human beings. A realistic period of time to evaluate such things more fully is perhaps a year, or several years. We need to be able to stick with the training, practising meditation and post-meditation every day for better or worse, in varying life circumstances over a long period of time, to determine if it is the right path for us.

Slogan Fifty-Four: Train Wholeheartedly

It is important not to waver in the training, but that is not enough. We also need to train wholeheartedly. It may be that we manage to maintain a daily discipline but still realize over time that the training has become half-hearted. If we realize that this is the case not only during temporary slumps, we need to seriously reflect on the situation and investigate why.

Perhaps we have lost touch with our original motivation and need to go back to the preparations summarized in the first of the slogans.

It may also be that we have emotional needs that we need to explore further. We may feel lonely, and long for friendship or someone to be close to. We may need to heal a wounded relationship or give an elderly parent more time and care than we currently do.

If we don't take such emotional needs seriously enough, they can affect us unconsciously and make the practice of compassion half-hearted. If we instead focus our attention on them and explore them deeply, they can become part of our training and thus make the training more wholehearted.

Slogan Fifty-Five: Free Yourself by Examining and Analyzing

We are encouraged to actively examine our weaknesses. In which situations are our ego defences activated, and how do these manifest? Which emotional reactions are dominant: greed, ill will, envy, miserliness, discontent, contempt? We don't have to beat ourselves up when we recognize such tendencies in ourselves. We are all affected by these mental poisons. We don't have to identify with them – instead we can see them as influences flowing through us and others. Although the poisons are unhealthy and have the potential to harm us and others, we can face them with kind acceptance and a sense of humour.

'Oops, I said something that might have sounded a bit patronizing. Am I being a bit arrogant right now?' Or: 'Wow, that sounded bitter. Do I feel bitter about the situation? Maybe.'

Once we have identified such reactive patterns and know that we can work with them, we can practise exposing ourselves to situations that provoke them, to get to know ourselves better and to actively work on changing these patterns. We can also meditate on and explore negative emotions to get to know and understand them better.

We can see how negative emotions arise depending on certain circumstances, but also how they dissolve without leaving anything behind. In this regard we can see that they are empty. They come from nowhere and then disappear into nothingness.

Exercise

Observe feelings and thoughts

It can be very valuable and rewarding to observe how emotions and thoughts arise and dissolve, both in meditation and in everyday life.

Take a short break from reading, and sit in silence for a while. Then think of a situation that usually provokes one of the mental toxins, such as greed, anger, or envy. How does your body feel when you think about this? What thoughts arise? Observe what happens in your body and mind when you dwell on this situation.

If you wish, you can also consciously seek out such a situation in your daily life, when you are not meditating, and observe your feelings and thoughts. What happens in the body and mind? Stop for a moment, and be aware of your body and breathing.

Then you can try just observing what is happening, and not act on the feelings. What happens then? Can you notice how emotions and thoughts arise, how they stay for a while, and how they then dissolve? How does it feel in your mind and body?

Slogan Fifty-Six: Don't Feel Sorry for Yourself

When faced with our own 'self-creating' and 'self-assertive' tendencies, it is easy to become overwhelmed. We can sometimes feel despondent and begin to doubt the whole project. Difficulties and setbacks can make us feel sorry for ourselves.

Instead of feeling sorry for ourselves, we should reflect with self-compassion on the difficult task we have taken on. It is difficult to overcome our deeply rooted self-centredness, and the reactive patterns and emotions associated with it. It is perhaps the most difficult thing a person can do.

But we also have access to the most effective and powerful methods available for self-transcendence, and can draw inspiration from a thousand-year-old lineage of people who have practised lojong and been successful.

If we practise lojong, there is no need to feel sorry for ourselves. Even if we suffer from misfortune or illness, we have access to teachings that can help us use our misfortune as a means of self-overcoming. We are truly fortunate, and the ones we should feel sorry for are all those who do not have the same opportunities.

Slogan Fifty-Seven: Don't Be Touchy

There are different versions of this slogan as well. To be touchy means to be easily offended and annoyed if you are not treated with due respect. Geshe Chekawa thinks of a lama who, despite his knowledge and qualifications, does not feel he is being treated with the reverence that tradition demands.

If we broaden the meaning a bit, this slogan includes all situations where we feel offended and insulted because others do not perceive our position in the social hierarchy as we do.

This is yet another expression of attachment to the self and something we need to let go of.

Others may have a patronizing attitude because they are unsympathetic and trapped in their own bubble of self-absorption. But being easily offended or annoyed is not helpful to either party. What we can ask for is to be treated with the same basic respect as everyone else. We cannot ask to be treated with special respect because we are more knowledgeable, more spiritually developed, or more special than others.

In all kinds of relationships it is important not to be overly touchy: in friendships and love relationships, as well as with work colleagues. We may feel slightly offended by a stray comment, but, unless it is obvious that it was meant to hurt, it is usually better to let it pass and to reflect on it when you are in a calm mood.

Slogan Fifty-Eight: Don't Be Frivolous

It is important that we do not become so serious in our training in wisdom and compassion that we lose touch with playfulness and humour. But we also need to watch out for the other extreme. If we tend to make jokes all the time and not take anything seriously, we can become tiresome to ourselves and others in the long run.

For some people, frivolity is a kind of defence, an excuse not to make life changes and break unhealthy habits. As soon as things heat up a little, they have a joke at hand or something to say that distracts from what is being talked about or what is happening.

Guidelines for Lojong

It is important to allow room for humour and self-detachment in our training, but it must be within the framework of a responsible and serious approach to life in general.

Traleg Kyabgon renders the slogan as, 'Don't be like an open book', or more literally, according to the Tibetan model, 'Don't let everyone see your feelings.' It is a form of frivolity to constantly give in to all feelings and display them outwardly. Many feelings are fleeting, and constantly expressing what we feel in the moment is not very helpful to others or, in the long run, to ourselves. A social-media version of this would be 'don't overshare'. Openness and honesty are important qualities, but as always it is a question of balance and good judgement, so that we know when it is appropriate to show our feelings and when it is better to keep them to ourselves.

Slogan Fifty-Nine: Don't Expect Applause

Imagine practising mindfulness, loving-kindness, and compassion for many years, perhaps five, ten, or twenty years. You inevitably experience ups and downs, but there are also breakthroughs with new insights and expansive feelings. You clearly notice how your own experience of life becomes richer and more satisfying. You also seem to notice that others around you are feeling better and handling life better, possibly through your influence.

But no one notices. No one gives you praise or appreciation for all the time and energy you put into developing mindfulness, wisdom, and compassion. Not even a God in heaven sees you and acknowledges you.

How does that feel? If it feels okay, you have practised in the right way, with the right motivation. Our need for affirmation is deeply human, but it is also an expression of the illusion of a separate self. When we truly see that we are all interconnected, that deep down there is not an 'I' and a 'you', but only a 'we', it is our collective progress that matters. What matters is that we are part of a world that is gradually becoming more aware, loving, and compassionate. And then we don't need applause.

Conclusion

We have now had a good look at the seven-point mind training and fifty-nine slogans. We hope you've found them inspiring, as we have, and that you might want to try practising them in your own life. As we have mentioned in the text, they become part of one's overall Dharma practice in a natural way over time. The best way to take things further is to find a community to practise with, and to create time and space in your life for this both rewarding and challenging practice.

We have now come to the end of our imaginary journey following in the footsteps of great masters like Atisha and Geshe Chekawa. If we put what we learn into practice, we may one day be able to feel what Geshe Chekawa expresses in his closing verses:

Concluding verses[26]

When the five degenerations occur,[27]
This is the way to transform them into the path of
    awakening.
It is the essence of the nectar of the oral instructions
Which were handed down from Serlingpa.[28]
After awakening the karma from previous training
And feeling greatly inspired,
I have ignored suffering and insults
And sought the instructions to tame ego-clinging.
Now, when I die, I will have no regrets.

Links to Other Mind-Training Resources

There are a number of helpful talks by members of the Triratna Buddhist Order on lojong and mind training:

Dhammadinna: 'Seven point mind training' (2008),
    https://tinyurl.com/SevenPointMindTraining
Vidyamala: 'Compassionate warrior training' (2022),
    https://tinyurl.com/CompassionateWarriorTraining
International Council: lecture series in India (2018), 'Eight verses for training the mind',
    https://tinyurl.com/EightVersesForTrainingTheMind
Subhuti: 'Eight verses for training the mind' (2004),
    https://tinyurl.com/EightVersesForTrainingTheMind2

Notes and References

1 See Sangharakshita, *Living with Kindness*, in *The Complete Works*, vol.15: *Pali Canon Teachings and Translations*, Windhorse Publications, Cambridge 2024, pp.245–345.
2 Jamgön Kongtrül, *The Great Path of Awakening*, trans. Ken McLeod, Shambhala, Boston, MA, 2005.
3 Dilgo Khyentse Rinpoche, *Enlightened Courage*, Snow Lion, Boulder, CO, 2006.
4 Chögyam Trungpa, *Training the Mind and Cultivating Loving-Kindness*, Shambhala, Boston, MA, 2003; *Pema Chödrön's Compassion Cards: Teachings for Awakening the Heart in Everyday Life*, Shambhala, Boulder, CO, 2016.
5 B. Alan Wallace, *The Seven-Point Mind Training*, Snow Lion, Boulder, CO, 2012.
6 Traleg Kyabgon, *The Practice of Lojong: Cultivating Compassion through Training the Mind*, Shambhala, Boston, MA, 2007.
7 Norman Fischer, *Training in Compassion: Zen Teachings on the Practice of Lojong*, Shambhala, Boulder, CO, 2012.
8 From the preliminaries of the *Tharpe Delam Mula Yogas*, translated from the Tibetan by Sangharakshita with the help of Dhardo Rinpoche, unpublished. This version is a rendering by Prakasha.
9 If you want to read more, we can recommend *Change Your Mind* by Paramananda, Windhorse Publications, Cambridge 2005. Viryabodhi has also recorded several guided meditations; see viryabodhi.se where there are links to Free Buddhist Audio, Insight Timer, and SoundCloud.
10 See for example: William S. Waldron, *The Buddhist Unconscious: The Alaya-Vijnana in the Context of Indian Buddhist Thought*, Taylor & Francis, London 2003.

Notes and References

11 The three basic poisons, in Sanskrit *kleshas*, are *raga*, *dvesa*, and *moha*. *Raga* means 'sensual desire' or 'greed'. *Dvesa* means 'aversion' or 'hatred'. *Moha* stands for a deep-seated unwillingness to see reality as it is, and is usually translated as 'ignorance', 'delusion', or, as here, 'unconsciousness'.

12 Read about these approaches in Sangharakshita, *Mind Reactive and Creative*, in *The Complete Works*, vol.6: *The Essential Sangharakshita*, Windhorse Publications, Cambridge 2024, pp.153–76.

13 These metaphysical 'bodies' are different aspects of the enlightened mind: *dharmakaya*, *sambhogakaya*, *nirmanakaya*, and *svabhavikakaya*. The *dharmakaya*, or 'body of truth', represents the innermost nature of the enlightened mind, which is emptiness and unmanifested potential. *Sambhogakaya*, or 'pleasure body', is the enlightened mind as spiritual energy and communication on a meditative level. The *nirmanakaya*, or 'manifestation body', is the embodiment of the enlightened mind, which we would all be able to see if we met a buddha. In addition to these three 'bodies', Indo-Tibetan Buddhism speaks of a fourth 'body', which is the *svabhavikakaya*, the 'essence body'. *Svabhavikakaya* should be understood not as a separate body from the other three, but as a unifying concept that indicates how the different bodies form an integrated whole.

14 Subpersonalities are referred to in Jungian psychology, psychosynthesis, and Internal Family Systems, among others. Compare for example Jung's idea of the Shadow, as a mainly unconscious aspect of our personality.

15 A supernatural being or spirit that accompanies a person in connection to their fate or fortune; comparable to the fetch of Irish folklore.

16 Jamgön Kongtrül, *The Great Path of Awakening*, p.23.

17 *Uposatha Sutta*, Udana 5.5, translated by John D. Ireland, available at https://www.accesstoinsight.org/tipitaka/kn/ud/ud.5.05.irel.html, accessed on 4 October 2024.

18 Natural morality can be said to be morality based on our ability to empathize with other living beings and a desire not to harm or otherwise cause suffering. It can be contrasted with

Notes and References

conventional morality, which involves codes of behaviour that are culturally determined. For example, in India it has been considered inappropriate for a man and a woman to hold hands in public, even if they are married, while it is more acceptable for two people of the same sex to do so. In Europe, the opposite has been the case, at least until recently. You can read more in *Not About Being Good* by Subhadramati, Windhorse Publications, Cambridge 2013.

19 Jetsun Milarepa (born around 1052, died around 1135) was one of Tibet's most famous yogis and poets. See *The Tibetan Book of Living and Dying*, Rider, London 1992, p.12.

20 Jamgön Kongtrül, *The Great Path of Awakening*, p.30.

21 The most famous precepts in Buddhism are the five precepts:
> I undertake the training principle to refrain from taking life.
> I undertake the training principle of refraining from taking the not-given.
> I undertake the training principle of abstaining from sexual misconduct.
> I undertake the training principle of refraining from false speech.
> I undertake the training principle of refraining from ingesting substances that cloud the mind.

These five precepts are complemented in Triratna by five 'positive precepts':
> With deeds of loving-kindness, I purify my body.
> With open-handed generosity, I purify my body.
> With stillness, simplicity, and contentment, I purify my body.
> With truthful communication, I purify my speech.
> With mindfulness clear and radiant, I purify my mind.

22 See note 11.

23 Dogen (1200–53) was a Japanese Zen Buddhist monk who is considered to have founded Soto, a school of Japanese Zen.

24 See note 12.

25 Arthur Schopenhauer (1788–1860) argues that we can choose what to do, but not what to want. You could extend this, and ask whether we can choose what to think or feel. Or do will,

thought, and feeling define what we are at any given moment? So that will, thought, and feeling choose us, rather than us choosing them? What we *can* do is to consciously observe how will, thoughts, and feelings arise. We can reinforce and act on what is in line with our overall purpose in life and allow other thoughts and feelings to arise and disappear, as all mental activity does, without reacting to them and without energizing them.

26 This translation was put together by Vessantara and Vijayamala in February 2021, based on other English versions and after consulting Lama Tilmann Lhundrup about the Tibetan.

27 The five degenerations are the degenerations of time, conscious beings, longevity, opinions, and mental poisons, which characterize *kaliyuga*, a period of general decay.

28 The name Serlingpa (in Tibetan) means 'from Suvarnadvipa', which is Sanskrit for 'the golden island', referring to Sumatra and the surrounding Indonesian islands. Serlingpa, or Dharmakirti as he was also known, taught Atisha for twelve years in Sumatra, and is considered to have laid the foundations of the lojong system.

WINDHORSE PUBLICATIONS

Windhorse Publications is a Buddhist charitable company based in the UK. Our books, which are distributed internationally, champion Buddhism, meditation, and mindfulness. They offer fresh interpretations of Buddhist teachings and their application to contemporary life, with subject matter and authors from across the Buddhist tradition, catering for a broad range of interest and experience. In addition to publishing titles exploring classic texts for modern audiences, we aspire to publish books that offer a Buddhist perspective on today's challenges, including social inequality, the environment and climate, gender, mental health, and more. Established in the 1970s to publish the writing of Urgyen Sangharakshita (1925–2018), the founder of the Triratna Buddhist Order, Windhorse Publications continues to be dedicated to preserving and keeping in print his impressive and influential body of work, making it accessible for future generations. As well as high-quality print and eBooks, Windhorse Publications produces accompanying audio, podcast, video, and teaching resources.

Windhorse Publications
38 Newmarket Road
Cambridge CB5 8DT
info@windhorsepublications.com

North America Distributors: Consortium Book Sales & Distribution
210 American Drive
Jackson TN 38301
USA
https://www.cbsd.com/

Australia and New Zealand Distributors: Windhorse Books
PO Box 574
Newtown NSW 2042
Australia
https://windhorse.com.au/books.html

THE TRIRATNA BUDDHIST COMMUNITY

Windhorse Publications is a part of the Triratna Buddhist Community, an international movement with centres in Europe, India, North and South America, and Australasia. At these centres, members of the Triratna Buddhist Order offer classes in meditation and Buddhism. Activities of the Triratna Community also include retreat centres, residential spiritual communities, ethical Right Livelihood businesses, and the Karuna Trust, a UK fundraising charity that supports social welfare projects in the slums and villages of India.

Through these and other activities, Triratna is developing a unique approach to Buddhism, not simply as a philosophy and a set of techniques, but as a creatively directed way of life for all people living in the conditions of the modern world.

If you would like more information about Triratna please visit thebuddhistcentre.com or write to:

London Buddhist Centre
51 Roman Road
London E2 0HU
UK
contact@lbc.org.uk

Aryaloka
14 Heartwood Circle
Newmarket NH 03857
USA
info@aryaloka.org

Sydney Buddhist Centre
24 Enmore Road
Sydney NSW 2042
Australia
info@sydneybuddhistcentre.org.au

Not About Being Good
A Practical Guide to Buddhist Ethics
Subhadramati

While there are numerous books on Buddhist meditation and philosophy, there are few books that are entirely devoted to the practice of Buddhist ethics. Subhadramati communicates clearly both their founding principles and the practical methods to embody them.

Buddhist ethics are not about conforming to a set of conventions, not about 'being good' in order to gain rewards. Instead, living ethically springs from the awareness that other people are no different from yourself. You can actively develop this awareness, through cultivating love, clarity, and contentment. Helping you to come into greater harmony with all that lives, this is ultimately your guidebook to a more satisfactory life.

In touch with the wonder of being alive, Subhadramati is a realistic and sympathetic guide to ethics in the twenty-first century. – Vidyamala Burch OBE, author of *Mindfulness for Health*

Writing with passion, humour, and delicacy, gloriously free from moralism, her aim is to help us live a richer and fuller life. – Maitreyabandhu, author of *Life with Full Attention*

Places ethics and meditation at the heart of Buddhist practice, and shows how they work together in transforming ordinary human beings into Buddhas. – Professor Damien Keown, author of *The Nature of Buddhist Ethics*

ISBN 9781 909314 01 6
176 pages

Life with Full Attention

A Practical Course in Mindfulness

Maitreyabandhu

In this eight-week course on mindfulness, Maitreyabandhu teaches you how to pay closer attention to experience. Each week he introduces a different aspect of mindfulness – such as awareness of the body, feelings, thoughts, and the environment – and recommends a number of easy practices; from trying out a simple meditation to reading a poem. Featuring personal stories, examples, and suggestions, *Life with Full Attention* is a valuable aid to mindfulness both as a starting point and for the more experienced.

ISBN 9781 899579 98 3
328 pages

Buddhist Meditation
Tranquillity, Imagination & Insight
Kamalashila

First published in 1991, this book is a comprehensive and practical guide to Buddhist meditation, providing a complete introduction for beginners, as well as detailed advice for experienced meditators seeking to deepen their practice. Kamalashila explores the primary aims of Buddhist meditation: enhanced awareness, true happiness, and – ultimately – liberating insight into the nature of reality. This third edition includes new sections on the importance of the imagination, on Just Sitting, and on reflection on the Buddha. Kamalashila has been teaching meditation since becoming a member of the Triratna Buddhist Order in 1974. He has developed approaches to meditation practice that are accessible to people in the contemporary world, whilst being firmly grounded in the Buddhist tradition.

A wonderfully practical and accessible introduction to the important forms of Buddhist meditation. From his years of meditation practice, Kamalashila has written a book useful for both beginners and longtime practitioners. – Gil Fronsdal, author of *A Monastery Within*, founder of the Insight Meditation Center, California, USA

This enhanced new edition guides readers more clearly into the meditations and draws out their significance more fully, now explicitly oriented around the 'system of meditation'. This system provides a fine framework both for understanding where various practices fit in and for reflecting on the nature of our own spiritual experiences. Kamalashila has also woven in an appreciation of a view of the nature of mind that in the Western tradition is known as the imagination, helping make an accessible link to our own philosophical and cultural traditions. – Lama Surya Das, author of *Awakening the Buddha Within*, founder of Dzogchen Center and Dzogchen Meditation Retreats, USA

His approach is a clear, thorough, honest, and, above all, open-ended exploration of the practical problems for those new to and even quite experienced in meditation. – Lama Shenpen Hookham, author of *There's More to Dying Than Death*, founder of the Awakened Heart Sangha, UK

Sailing the Worldly Winds
A Buddhist Way through the Ups and Downs of Life
Vajragupta

How do we really get on in this world? Tossed around by gain, buffeted by loss, borne aloft by praise, cast down by blame, how can we not be ground under, lose all direction, confidence, and sense of purpose? The Buddha had clear guidance on how to rise above these 'worldly winds', and Vajragupta here opens up for us the Buddha's compassionate yet uncompromising teaching.

Using reflections, exercises, and suggestions for daily practice, this book can help you find greater equanimity and perspective in the ups and downs – big and small – of everyday life.

ISBN 978 1 9073141 0 0
128 pages

Notes

www.ingramcontent.com/pod-product-compliance
Lightning Source LLC
Chambersburg PA
CBHW072055110526
44590CB00018B/3189